YOUR PERSONAL

ASTROLOGY

PLANNER

VIRGO
2010

YOUR PERSONAL

ASTROLOGY

PLANNER

VIRGO
2010

RICK LEVINE **& JEFF** JAWER

STERLING

New York / London
www.sterlingpublishing.com

STERLING and the distinctive Sterling logo are registered
trademarks of Sterling Publishing Co., Inc.

2 4 6 8 10 9 7 5 3 1

Published by Sterling Publishing Co., Inc.
387 Park Avenue South, New York, NY 10016
© 2009 Sterling Publishing Co., Inc.
Text © 2009 Rick Levine and Jeff Jawer
Distributed in Canada by Sterling Publishing
C/o Canadian Manda Group, 165 Dufferin Street,
Toronto, Ontario, Canada M6K 3H6
Distributed in the United Kingdom by GMC Distribution Services
Castle Place, 166 High Street, Lewes, East Sussex, England BN7 1XU
Distributed in Australia by Capricorn Link (Australia) Pty. Ltd.
P.O. Box 704, Windsor, NSW 2756, Australia

Sterling ISBN 978-1-4027-6413-4

For information about custom editions, special sales, premium and
corporate purchases, please contact Sterling Special Sales
Department at 800-805-5489 or
specialsales@sterlingpublishing.com.

TABLE OF CONTENTS

THE PURPOSE OF THIS BOOK

The more you learn about yourself, the better able you are to wisely use the energies in your life. For more than 3,000 years, astrology has been the sharpest tool in the box for describing the human condition. Used by virtually every culture on the planet, astrology continues to serve as a link between individual lives and planetary cycles. We gain valuable insights into personal issues with a birth chart, and can plot the patterns of the year ahead in meaningful ways for individuals as well as groups. You share your sun sign with eight percent of humanity. Clearly, you're not all going to have the same day, even if the basic astrological cycles are the same. Your individual circumstances, the specific factors of your entire birth chart, and your own free will help you write your unique story.

The purpose of this book is to describe the energies of the Sun, Moon, and planets for the year ahead and help you create your future, rather than being a victim of it. We aim to facilitate your journey by showing you the turns ahead in the road of life and hopefully the best ways to navigate them.

YOU ARE THE STAR
OF YOUR LIFE

It is not our goal to simply predict events. Rather, we are reporting the planetary energies—the cosmic weather in which you are living—so that you understand these conditions and know how to use them most effectively.

The power, though, isn't in the stars, but in your mind, your heart, and the choices that you make every day. Regardless of how strongly you are buffeted by the winds of change or bored by stagnation, you have many ways to view any situation. Learning about the energies of the Sun, Moon, and planets will both sharpen and widen your perspective, thereby giving you additional choices.

The language of astrology is a gift of awareness, not a rigid set of rules. It works best when blended with common sense, intuition, and self-trust. This is your life, and no one knows how to live it as well as you. Take what you need from this book and leave the rest. Although the planets set the stage for the year ahead, you're the writer, director, and star of your life and you can play the part in whatever way you choose. *Your Personal Astrology Planner* uses information about your sun sign to give you a better understanding of how the planetary waves will wash upon your shore. We each navigate our lives through time, and each moment has unique qualities. Astrology gives us the ability to describe the constantly changing timescape. For example, if you know the trajectory and the speed of an approaching storm, you can choose to delay a leisurely afternoon sail on the bay, thus avoiding an unpleasant situation.

By reading this book, you can improve your ability to align with the cosmic weather, the larger patterns that affect you day to day. You can become more effective by aligning with the cosmos and cocreating the year ahead with a better understanding of the energies around you.

Astrology doesn't provide quick fixes to life's complex issues. It doesn't offer neatly packed black-and-white answers in a world filled with an infinite variety of shapes and colors. It can, however, give you a much clearer picture of the invisible forces influencing your life.

ENERGY & EVENTS

Two sailboats can face the same gale yet travel in opposite directions as a result of how the sails are positioned. Similarly, how you respond to the energy of a particular set of circumstances may be more responsible for your fate than the given situation itself. We delineate the energetic winds for your year ahead, but your attitude shapes the unfolding events, and your responses alter your destiny.

This book emphasizes the positive, not because all is good, but because astrology shows us ways to transform even the power of a storm into beneficial results. Empowerment comes from learning to see the invisible energy patterns that impact the visible landscape as you fill in the details of your story every day on this spinning planet, orbited by the Moon, lit by the Sun, and colored by the nuances of the planets.

You are a unique point in an infinite galaxy of unlimited possibilities, and the choices that you make have consequences. So use this book in a most magical way to consciously improve your life.

MOON CHARTS

2010 NEW MOONS

Each New Moon marks the beginning of a cycle. In general, this is the best time to plant seeds for future growth. Use the days preceeding the New Moon to finish old business prior to starting what comes next. The focused mind can be quite sharp during this phase. Harness the potential of the New Moon by stating your intentions—out loud or in writing—for the weeks ahead. Hold these goals in your mind; help them grow to fruition through conscious actions as the Moon gains light during the following two weeks. In the chart below, the dates and times refer to when the Moon and Sun align in each zodiac sign (see p16), initiating a new lunar cycle.

DATE	TIME	SIGN
January 15	2:11 AM EST	Capricorn **(ECLIPSE)**
February 13	9:51 PM EST	Aquarius
March 15	5:01 PM EDT	Pisces
April 14	8:28 AM EDT	Aries
May 13	9:04 PM EDT	Taurus
June 12	7:14 AM EDT	Gemini
July 11	3:40 PM EDT	Cancer **(ECLIPSE)**
August 9	11:08 PM EDT	Leo
September 8	6:29 AM EDT	Virgo
October 7	2:44 PM EDT	Libra
November 6	12:51 AM EDT	Scorpio
December 5	12:35 PM EST	Sagittarius

2010 FULL MOONS

The Full Moon reflects the light of the Sun as subjective feelings reflect the objective events of the day. Dreams seem bigger; moods feel stronger. The emotional waters run with deeper currents. This is the phase of culmination, a turning point in the energetic cycle. Now it's time to listen to the inner voices. Rather than starting new projects, the two weeks after the Full Moon are when we complete what we can and slow our outward expressions in anticipation of the next New Moon. In this chart, the dates and times refer to when the moon is opposite the sun in each zodiac sign, marking the emotional peak of each lunar cycle.

DATE	TIME	SIGN
January 30	1:17 AM EST	Leo
February 28	11:37 AM EST	Virgo
March 29	10:25 PM EDT	Libra
April 28	8:18 AM EDT	Scorpio
May 27	7:07 PM EDT	Sagittarius
June 26	7:30 AM EDT	Capricorn **(ECLIPSE)**
July 25	9:36 PM EDT	Aquarius
August 24	1:04 PM EDT	Pisces
September 23	5:17 AM EDT	Aries
October 22	9:36 PM EDT	Aries
November 21	12:27 PM EST	Taurus
December 21	3:13 AM EST	Gemini **(ECLIPSE)**

ASTROLOGY, YOU & THE WORLD

WELCOME TO YOUR SUN SIGN

The Sun, Moon, and Earth and all the planets lie within a plane called the **ecliptic** and move through a narrow band of stars made up by 12 constellations called the **zodiac**. The Earth revolves around the Sun once a year, but from our point of view, it appears that the Sun moves through each sign of the zodiac for one month. There are 12 months and astrologically there are 12 signs. The astrological months, however, do not match our calendar, and start between the 19th and 23rd of each month. Everyone is born to an astrological month, like being born in a room with a particular perspective of the world. Knowing your sun sign provides useful information about your personality and your future, but for a more detailed astrological analysis, a full birth chart calculation based on your precise date, time, and place of birth is necessary. Get your complete birth chart online at:

http://www.tarot.com/astrology/astroprofile

This book is about your zodiac sign. Your Sun in the earth sign of efficient Virgo is analytical and practical. You excel at separating the wheat from the chaff, the valuable kernel from the rest. As such, you can be highly discriminating, even critical. You're a careful perfectionist in your work. Your greatest strength is being able to apply what you know to serve others. More than anything, you want to be useful.

THE PLANETS

We refer to the Sun and Moon as planets. Don't worry; we do know about modern astronomy. Although the Sun is really a star and the Moon is a satellite, they are called planets for astrological purposes. The astrological planets are the Sun, the Moon, Mercury, Venus, Mars, Jupiter, Saturn, Chiron, Uranus, Neptune, and Pluto.

Your sun sign is the most obvious astrological placement, for the Sun returns to the same sign every year. But at the same time, the Moon is orbiting the Earth, changing signs every two and a third days. Mercury, Venus, and Mars each move through a sign in a few weeks to a few months.

Jupiter spends a whole year in a sign—and Pluto visits a sign for up to 30 years! The ever-changing positions of the planets alter the energetic terrain through which we travel. The planets are symbols; each has a particular range of meanings. For example, Venus is the goddess of love, but it really symbolizes beauty in a spectrum of experiences. Venus can represent romantic love, sensuality, the arts, or good food. It activates anything that we value, including personal possessions and even money. To our ancestors, the planets actually animated life on Earth. In this way of thinking, every beautiful flower contains the essence of Venus.

Each sign has a natural affinity to an individual planet, and as this planet moves through the sky, it sends messages of particular interest to people born under that sign. Your key or ruling planet is Mercury, the Messenger of the Heavens. Quicksilver Mercury is the fastest of the true planets, symbolic of the speed and changeability of thought. Its movement shows the qualities of your thinking process and speech. Planets can be described by many different words, for the mythology of each is a rich tapestry. In this book we use a variety of words when talking about each planet in order to convey the most applicable meaning. The table below describes a few keywords for each planet, including the Sun and Moon.

PLANET	SYMBOL	KEYWORDS
Sun	☉	Consciousness, Will, Vitality
Moon	☽	Subconscious, Emotions, Habits
Mercury	☿	Communication, Thoughts, Transportation
Venus	♀	Desire, Love, Money, Values
Mars	♂	Action, Physical Energy, Drive
Jupiter	♃	Expansion, Growth, Optimism
Saturn	♄	Contraction, Maturity, Responsibility
Chiron	⚷	Healing, Pain, Subversion
Uranus	♅	Awakening, Unpredictable, Inventive
Neptune	♆	Imagination, Spirituality, Confusion
Pluto	♇	Passion, Intensity, Regeneration

HOUSES

Just as planets move through the signs of the zodiac, they also move through the houses in an individual chart. The 12 houses correspond to the 12 signs, but are individualized, based upon your sign. In this book we use Solar Houses, which place your sun sign in your 1st House. Therefore, when a planet enters a new sign it also enters a new house. If you know your exact time of birth, the rising sign determines the 1st House. You can learn your rising sign by entering your birth date at:

http://www.tarot.com/astrology/astroprofile

HOUSE	SIGN	KEYWORDS
1st House	Aries	Self, Appearance, Personality
2nd House	Taurus	Possessions, Values, Self-Worth
3rd House	Gemini	Communication, Siblings, Short Trips
4th House	Cancer	Home, Family, Roots
5th House	Leo	Love, Romance, Children, Play
6th House	Virgo	Work, Health, Daily Routines
7th House	Libra	Marriage, Relationships, Business Partners
8th House	Scorpio	Intimacy, Transformation, Shared Resources
9th House	Sagittarius	Travel, Higher Education, Philosophy
10th House	Capricorn	Career, Community, Ambition
11th House	Aquarius	Groups and Friends, Associations, Social Ideals
12th House	Pisces	Imagination, Spirituality, Secret Activities

ASPECTS

As the planets move through the sky in their various cycles, they form ever-changing angles with one another. Certain angles create significant geometric shapes. So, when two planets are 90 degrees apart, they conform to a square; 60 degrees of separation conforms to a sextile, or six-pointed star. Planets create **aspects** when they're at these special angles. Aspects explain how the individual symbolism of pairs of planets combine into an energetic pattern.

ASPECT	DEGREES	KEYWORDS
Conjunction	0	Compression, Blending, Focus
Opposition	180	Tension, Awareness, Balance
Trine	120	Harmony, Free-Flowing, Ease
Square	90	Resistance, Stress, Dynamic Conflict
Quintile	72	Creativity, Metaphysical, Magic
Sextile	60	Support, Intelligent, Activating
Quincunx	150	Irritation, Annoyance, Adjustment

2010 GENERAL FORECAST:
THE INDIVIDUAL AND THE COLLECTIVE

Astrology works for individuals, groups, and even for humanity as a whole. You will have your own story in 2010, but it will unfold among nearly seven billion other tales of human experience. We are each unique, yet our lives touch one another; our destinies are woven together by weather and war, by the economy, science, music, politics, religion, and all the other threads of life on planet Earth. We make personal choices every day, yet great events are beyond the control of anyone. When a town is flooded, it affects everyone, yet personal astrology patterns will describe the specific response of each person. Our existence is both an individual and a collective experience.

We are living in a time when the tools of self-awareness fill books, TV and radio shows, Web sites, podcasts, newspapers, and DVDs, and we benefit greatly from them. Yet despite of all this wisdom, conflicts cause enormous suffering every day. Understanding personal issues is a powerful means for increasing happiness, but knowledge of our collective issues is equally important for our safety, sanity, and well-being. This astrological look at the major trends and planetary patterns for 2010 provides a framework for comprehending the potentials and challenges we face together, so that we can advance with tolerance and respect as a community and fulfill our potential as individuals.

The astrological events used for this forecast are the transits of major planets Jupiter and Saturn, the retrograde cycles of Mercury, and the eclipses of the Sun and the Moon.

A NOTE ABOUT THE DATES IN THIS BOOK

All events are based upon the Eastern Time Zone of the United States. Because of local time differences, an event occurring just a few minutes after midnight in the East will actually happen the prior day in the rest of the country. Although the key dates are the exact dates of any particular alignment, some of you are so ready for certain things to happen that you can react to a transit a day or two before it is exact. And sometimes you can be so entrenched in habits or unwilling to change that you may not notice the effects right away. Allow extra time around each key date to feel the impact of any event.

JUPITER IN PISCES:
WILD WAVES OF CHANGE
January 17, 2010–June 6, 2010
September 9, 2010–January 22, 2011

Jupiter, the planet of expansion, reconnects us with our spiritual roots in its watery home sign of Pisces. Knowledge is no longer an intellectual abstraction; it is a living experience that comes from our connection to the cosmos. Imagination is stronger now as the limits of logic are dissolved in the boundless waters of intuition, which seem to reveal answers to all life's questions. The great gift of Jupiter in Pisces is that wisdom is equally available to everyone. The challenge, though, is connecting the grand vision that inspires us with the specific steps required to turn it into reality. Fortunately, Jupiter's foray into action-oriented Aries provides the fire to set concepts into motion.

JUPITER IN ARIES:
A GLIMPSE OF THE FUTURE
June 6, 2010–September 9, 2010
January 22, 2011–June 4, 2011

A new day dawns with farseeing Jupiter in pioneering Aries. The urge to test ideas on the battlefield of experience amplifies impatience yet rewards individuals and institutions willing to take risks. Breakthroughs in energy generation are now possible. Innovations in education and travel are likely to follow. However, a lack of compromise on ideological matters can increase the potential for conflict. Bold statements and actions provoke rapid responses, reducing the effectiveness of diplomacy. Jupiter's stressful aspects with Saturn, Uranus, and Pluto may pit progressive forces against those who resist change. On the positive side, new ways of seeing ourselves can quickly break down old barriers, allowing our common humanity to overcome the differences of nationality, ideology, religion, gender, and race.

SATURN IN VIRGO:
HEALTHY VIGILANCE
September 2, 2007–October 29, 2009
April 7, 2010–July 21, 2010

Saturn, the planet of boundaries and limitations, takes twenty-nine years to orbit the Sun and pass through all twelve signs of the zodiac. It demands serious responsibility, reveals the work necessary to overcome obstacles, and teaches us how to structure our lives. Saturn thrives on patience and commitment, rewarding well-planned and persistent effort while punishing sloppiness and procrastination with disappointment, delay, and even failure.

Saturn's passage through methodical Virgo is a time to perfect skills, cut waste, and develop healthier habits. Virgo is less interested in unrestrained consumerism than in acquiring useful things. This opens the door to a new era of less conspicuous consumption and shifts the economy away from purchases of SUVs, big homes, and luxury items. Issues relating to impure food and water have already been in the news, with outbreaks of salmonella and E. coli poisoning raising wider concerns about contamination and urging us to improve our diets. Environmental concerns continue to escalate as we approach a critical point in the relationship between humanity and planet Earth. Fortunately, Saturn in exacting Virgo is also excellent for cleaning up unhealthy toxins produced by old technologies and building new ecologically friendly systems for the future.

SATURN IN LIBRA:
SURGE OF DIPLOMACY
October 29, 2009–April 7, 2010
July 21, 2010–October 5, 2012

Saturn's shift into peace-loving Libra marks a new chapter in all kinds of relationships, but there's some tough work to be done before harmony can be achieved. Saturn in Libra marks a time of significant legal changes when the scales of justice are recalibrated. The famous *Brown v. Board of Education* case—critical to reversing segregation in the United States—was launched in 1951 with Saturn in Libra. During this cycle, the legal definition of marriage is under reconsideration as we weigh and balance the spreading acceptance of same-sex marriages against the more traditional approach. The US Fairness Doctrine, which requires broadcasters to present contrasting views regarding controversial issues of public interest, could come up for scrutiny. Even challenges to international treaties governing war and peace can be expected.

When Saturn in Libra functions at its best, cooperation and civility allow diplomacy to flourish as reason replaces force. The need to weigh both sides of any argument can slow personal and public dialogue, yet it's worth the price to build bridges over seemingly impassable chasms. The negative side of Saturn, though, is its potential for rigidity, which can manifest now as a stubborn unwillingness to listen. Resistance to opposing points of view is simply an opportunity to test their worth; only with careful consideration can they be properly evaluated. Responsible individuals and wise leaders recognize the importance of treating others with respect as a foundation for any healthy relationship.

MERCURY RETROGRADES
**December 26, 2009–January 15, 2010 in Capricorn /
April 18–May 11 in Taurus / August 20–September 12
in Virgo / December 10 in Capricorn,
Direct December 30 in Sagittarius**

All true planets appear to move backward from time to time, because we view them from the moving platform of Earth. The most significant retrograde cycles are those of Mercury, the communication planet. Occurring three or four times a year for roughly three weeks at a time, these are periods when difficulties with travel, communication, details, and technical matters are likely.

Although many people think that Mercury's retrograde is negative, you can make this cycle work for you. Because personal and commercial interactions are emphasized, you can actually accomplish more than usual, especially if you stay focused on what needs to be done rather than initiating new projects. Still, you may feel as if you're treading water—or worse, carried backward in an undertow of unfinished business. Worry less about making progress than about the quality of your work. Pay extra attention to all your communication exchanges. Avoiding misunderstandings and omissions is the ideal way to minimize complications. Retrograde Mercury is best used to tie up loose ends as you review, redo, reconsider, and, in general, revisit the past.

This year, all four retrogrades begin in practical earth signs (Capricorn, Taurus, Virgo), challenging us to redefine our material values, ambitions, and methods. Sticking to literal interpretations of reality during these periods can be extremely limiting. We are pushed to question our perceptions and break the forms of recognition and description that bind us to our current ways of seeing and communicating. Intuitive approaches in which the subjective qualities of life take on more importance fill in the gaps where objective analyses fall short.

ECLIPSES
Solar: January 15 and July 11
Lunar: June 26 and December 21

Solar and Lunar Eclipses are special New and Full
Moons that indicate significant changes for individuals
and groups. They are powerful markers of events with
influences that can appear up to three months in
advance and last up to six months afterward.

January 15, Solar Eclipse in Capricorn:
Fall from Grace

The powerful changes of this eclipse are softened by its close conjunction with gentle Venus. Heads of state—especially female—may fall, but they're likely to land in cushy places with the planet of love and rewards in the picture. A supportive sextile from inventive Uranus encourages alternative forms of leadership and helpful shakeups in large organizations. This eclipse is visible through the middle of China, the southern tip of India, and Central Africa, making its impact stronger in these areas.

June 26, Lunar Eclipse in Capricorn:
Sudden Exposure

This Lunar Eclipse is conjunct insatiable Pluto, indicating major issues that threaten safety and security. Abuse of power is likely, especially in traditional institutions that have long resisted reform and exposure to public scrutiny. Toxicity can be a concern with Pluto's presence, perhaps affecting food supplies. The volatile conjunction of Jupiter and Uranus square the eclipse may precipitate rapid changes that unexpectedly undermine the viability of influential organizations. Positively, a healthy purge can restore life to fading companies and failing governments.

July 11, Solar Eclipse in Cancer:
Water Works

The potential for problems is considerable with this
Total Eclipse of the Sun conjunct the karmic South
Node of the Moon. Water may be threatened by pollution
or become threatening itself through storms and flood-
ing. Fortunately, Mars in efficient Virgo forms an intelligent sextile to the eclipse that provides rapid responses
whenever corrective action is needed. The vast majority
of the path of visibility falls over water in the South
Pacific, reducing its area of influence. It does touch the
southern tip of South America, where its effects may be
more evident.

December 21, Lunar Eclipse in Gemini:
Static on the Line

Tranquility on the home front and travel for the holidays
may be disturbed by this Total Lunar Eclipse in the
chatty transportation sign of Gemini. Intense Pluto and
talkative Mercury oppose the Moon, triggering provoca-
tive conversations and communication breakdowns. The
Jupiter-Uranus conjunction squares the eclipse, adding
another degree of instability that could trigger earth-
quakes or unusual weather. Still, brilliant ideas can
explode from unexpected sources to drastically shift
our perceptions and the ways in which we connect with
one another.

THE BOTTOM LINE:
SAVE THE HUMANS

All the talk about transformational shifts in 2010 at the supposed end of the Mayan calendar overlooks the incredible planetary forces that will reshape the future of humanity this year. Undoubtedly there will be major changes during slow-moving Uranus-Pluto squares of 2012–2015, reawakening the energy of the mid-1960s when revolutionary Uranus conjoined evolutionary Pluto. But we don't need to wait until then—when it may be too late—to start the work that so desperately needs to be done. The formative forces of the outer planets aligning at the beginning of the cardinal signs in 2010 suggest that the new era is opening now. The movements of expansive Jupiter and structuring Saturn from season-ending mutable signs where old energy is released to the initiating signs of Aries and Libra are enough by themselves to tell the tale of an emerging new world order.

Our least viable option, and most unlikely scenario, is standing still in a futile attempt to maintain the status quo. The year 2010 is not one of stagnation; it's a year when the slow simmer of unresolved issues boils over and demands our attention. The degree of stress is high, yet the potential for finally making the structural changes and sacrifices necessary to save humanity does exist. This is, happily, not some dreary trudge toward inevitable failure, but a turning point when the pressure of physical stress crosses with the genius of human potential to take us on a healthier and more hopeful path to the future.

Remember that all these astrological events are part of the general cosmic weather of the year, but will affect us each differently based on our individual astrological signs.

VIRGO
AUGUST–DECEMBER
2009 OVERVIEW

ANALYTICAL MIND

Your thinking grows sharper as intellectual Mercury enters discerning Virgo on **August 2**. The narrowing lens of perception helps you cut through complex issues to get at key points, increasing your efficiency and ability to influence others. Still, it's helpful to step back and widen your perspective occasionally to make sure that your precisely defined picture fits into the larger scheme of things. The Full Moon on **August 5** is a Lunar Eclipse in unconventional Aquarius that falls in your 6th House of Health, Work, and Daily Routines, reminding you that new ideas and systems aren't always better than old ones. Fortunately, active Mars in flexible Gemini trines the Moon to show you how to make adjustments without making waves.

Finding balance between tomorrow's potential and today's reality can seem challenging with a clumsy quincunx between positive Jupiter and pragmatic Saturn on **August 19**. This second in a series of three aspects—which began on **March 22** and finishes on **February 5, 2010**— requires you to play the role of a skeptic to overly enthusiastic believers as well as act as a source of inspiration for those stuck in doubt and fear. Connecting with your inner guides and having faith in your vision of a brighter future are possibilities with the New Moon in expressive Leo on **August 20**. This energizing event occurs in your 12th House of Privacy, where its flames of creativity may be hidden from view. Nourish your hopes quietly instead of sharing them too soon. The Sun's entry into hardworking Virgo on **August 22** will put some wind into your sails. This solar energy in your sign increases confidence and vitality to enrich your personal life and empower you in business.

SATURDAY 1 ★ Strong emotions are agitated today

SUNDAY 2 ★

MONDAY 3 ★

TUESDAY 4

WEDNESDAY 5   ○

THURSDAY 6

FRIDAY 7

SATURDAY 8

SUNDAY 9

MONDAY 10 ★ Slow down and concentrate on one task at a time

TUESDAY 11

WEDNESDAY 12

THURSDAY 13 ★ Your creativity is nourished with confidence

FRIDAY 14 ★

SATURDAY 15

SUNDAY 16

MONDAY 17 ★ **SUPER NOVA DAYS** Support comes from unexpected sources

---

TUESDAY 18 ★

WEDNESDAY 19

THURSDAY 20   ●

FRIDAY 21

SATURDAY 22

SUNDAY 23

MONDAY 24

TUESDAY 25 ★ Prepare for lasting breakthroughs of awareness

WEDNESDAY 26 ★

THURSDAY 27

FRIDAY 28

SATURDAY 29

SUNDAY 30

MONDAY 31

★ designates key date

RELATIONSHIPS
IN THE BALANCE

Examining relationships to balance with healthy self-interest and loving concern for others is a major theme for you this month. The Full Moon in psychic Pisces on **September 4** occurs in your 7th House of Partnerships, shedding new light on the subject. This compassionate water sign can open the way to richer emotional connections. Remember, however, that losing yourself to co-dependency is not a recipe for long-term success. Objective thinking is challenged when Mercury the Messenger turns retrograde on **September 7**. Your orderly world can be skewed by miscommunication and difficulty with details until your ruling planet turns direct again on **September 29**. Its backward turn starts in Libra in your 2nd House of Resources, indicating a potential review of your financial situation. On **September 17**, Mercury returns to your sign, making you more conscious of your appearance and attitude. Your flaws may seem more serious than is really the case, so even minor changes will have an impact.

The ongoing planetary tug-of-war between strict Saturn and rebellious Uranus flares up on **September 15** when they oppose each other again. This long series of aspects falls in your 1st House of Self and 7th House of Others, putting a strain on relationships. The New Moon in fussy Virgo on **September 18** triggers both planets as it joins Saturn and opposes Uranus, making you itchy for change—or desperate to stay put while a partner or close ally is anxious to make a move. Attractive Venus enters Virgo on **September 20**, swinging the balance in your favor by helping you recognize your true worth. The Sun enters cooperative Libra on **September 22**, marking the Autumnal Equinox and illuminating gifts of beauty and harmony in your 2nd House of Resources.

TUESDAY 1	
WEDNESDAY 2	
THURSDAY 3 ★ Controlling a situation or denying your feelings only increases tension	

FRIDAY 4 ★ ○

SATURDAY 5

SUNDAY 6

MONDAY 7

TUESDAY 8

WEDNESDAY 9

THURSDAY 10

FRIDAY 11 ★ Act on your desires: romance, play, and creativity

SATURDAY 12 ★

SUNDAY 13

MONDAY 14

TUESDAY 15

WEDNESDAY 16

THURSDAY 17 ★ It's a volatile time—saying less is better

FRIDAY 18 ●

SATURDAY 19

SUNDAY 20 ★ **SUPER NOVA DAYS** You are especially clear in your thinking

MONDAY 21 ★

TUESDAY 22 ★

WEDNESDAY 23 ★

THURSDAY 24

FRIDAY 25

SATURDAY 26

SUNDAY 27

MONDAY 28

TUESDAY 29

WEDNESDAY 30

MINING FOR GOLD

Money matters steal the spotlight this month as the New and Full Moons fall in your houses of finance. The initiating Aries Full Moon occurs on **October 4**, stimulating ideas about investments and business partnerships in your 8th House of Shared Resources. Take the lead in a current economic union, or consider starting a new one. Friends or colleagues should be good sources of information about ways to get a greater return on your time, money, and energy. The New Moon in artistic Libra lands in your 2nd House of Possessions on **October 18**, providing a more objective picture of your financial situation. Saturn enters Libra on **October 29** to crystallize material issues during the next two years. Draw on the undeveloped gifts you already have within you. You have creative skills that can be honed with patience and discipline to upgrade your sense of self-worth—and perhaps your income as well.

Intelligent Mercury provides a sharp perspective to values and resources when it enters your 2nd House on **October 9**. You may tend toward indecisiveness with this thoughtful planet in the consensus-seeking sign of Libra. Consulting with others who recognize your talent can give you a boost, but don't let someone else's negative opinion overrule your own best instincts. Auspicious Jupiter turns direct in your 6th House of Work on **October 12**, raising your hopes for more rewarding employment. If the vision of greater fulfillment on the job seems beyond your reach, don't give up. Your success will be a benefit to others. Once you take the next step, support is likely to come from unexpected sources.

THURSDAY 1 ★ Brilliant ideas are electrified in your mind

FRIDAY 2 ★

SATURDAY 3 ★

SUNDAY 4 ★ ○

MONDAY 5

TUESDAY 6

WEDNESDAY 7

THURSDAY 8 ★ **SUPER NOVA DAYS** Work and pleasure are blended in a rewarding way

FRIDAY 9 ★

SATURDAY 10 ★

SUNDAY 11

MONDAY 12

TUESDAY 13

WEDNESDAY 14 ★ Use your intuitive awareness to change your life

THURSDAY 15 ★

FRIDAY 16 ★

SATURDAY 17

SUNDAY 18 ●

MONDAY 19

TUESDAY 20 ★ You deliver information effectively on the job and in practical situations

WEDNESDAY 21

THURSDAY 22

FRIDAY 23

SATURDAY 24

SUNDAY 25

MONDAY 26

TUESDAY 27

WEDNESDAY 28 ★ Joy and generosity are present

THURSDAY 29 ★

FRIDAY 30

SATURDAY 31

STUDENT OF LIFE

Travel and education are key this month. The earthy
Taurus Full Moon on **November 2** falls in your 9th House of
Higher Thought and Faraway Places, inspiring you to seek
peace in a belief system or comfort in a distant land. You
need a break from the pressures of your regular routine.
Whether you plan a trip to the Caribbean, take a medita-
tion class, or schedule a daily iPod moment to tune out the
world, be sure to create space for yourself. Assertive Mars
in your 12th House of Privacy squares this Sun-Moon
opposition, telling you that you may have to struggle to get
what you want, so don't be timid in pursuit of your dreams.
Your ruling planet, Mercury, enters restless Sagittarius in
your 4th House of Roots on **November 15**. An urge to know
the truth about your family and its past evokes questions
that require honest answers. Blunt statements can clear
away cobwebs of confusion at home, but could also drive
others away if too abrasive.

The New Moon in passionate Scorpio on **November 16**
falls in your 3rd House of Information and Education. Its
message is that you need to learn more and communicate
with greater force. The intensity of this lunation is ampli-
fied by a powerful Saturn-Pluto square on **November 15**
that will return on **January 31, 2010**, and **August 21, 2010**.
Both planets demand that you concentrate to avoid feeling
overwhelmed by circumstances beyond your control.
Eliminate distractions, dig in and do research to find key
ideas, and apply what you discover with precision. The
Sun's entry into adventurous Sagittarius on **November 21**
stokes the fire in your belly, encouraging you to step out of
your comfort zone and aim higher in your life.

SUNDAY 1 ★ Emotional tides lead to breakthroughs in awareness

MONDAY 2 ★ ○

TUESDAY 3

WEDNESDAY 4

THURSDAY 5 ★ **SUPER NOVA DAYS** Ideas about relationships, self-worth, and personal values are challenged

FRIDAY 6 ★

SATURDAY 7 ★

SUNDAY 8 ★

MONDAY 9

TUESDAY 10

WEDNESDAY 11 ★ Don't lose track of the brilliant solutions you just discovered

THURSDAY 12

FRIDAY 13

SATURDAY 14

SUNDAY 15

MONDAY 16 ●

TUESDAY 17

WEDNESDAY 18

THURSDAY 19

FRIDAY 20

SATURDAY 21 ★ Letting go of a complicated plan will reduce stress

SUNDAY 22

MONDAY 23

TUESDAY 24

WEDNESDAY 25

THURSDAY 26

FRIDAY 27

SATURDAY 28

SUNDAY 29 ★ A flash of genius solves problems in unexpected ways

MONDAY 30 ★

SURPRISE ENDING

You must regroup, adjust your plans, and reorganize your life, for this transitional month features two Full Moons (one of them an eclipse), retrograde turns by Mars and Mercury, and the last of Jupiter's three magical conjunctions with Neptune and Chiron. On **December 2**, the Full Moon in verbal Gemini lights up your 10th House of Career, strengthening your communication skills and helping you make new connections. The danger of overextending yourself is reduced by steady Saturn's supportive trine to the Moon, enabling you to skillfully manage a busy schedule. Philosophical Jupiter joins healing Chiron on **December 7** and spiritual Neptune on **December 21** in the last of a series of conjunctions that began in May. This inspiring trio adds vision to your 6th House of Health and Daily Routines, lightening your load with imagination and idealism and pointing the way to more fulfilling work.

Domestic matters take the spotlight with a free-spirited Sagittarius New Moon in your 4th House of Roots on **December 16**. A tense square from erratic Uranus may create sudden chaos on the home front, but shaking the family tree unhooks you from old unhealthy patterns and opens the way to bigger dreams for tomorrow. Militant Mars starts marching backward in your 12th House of Secrets on **December 20**, energizing you with inner motivation well into next year. Turning anger into a creative plan is imperative if you hope to avoid resentment that could simmer dangerously for weeks. Mercury's retrograde shift on **December 26** ends the year on an introspective note. The moody Cancer Full Moon on **December 31** is a Lunar Eclipse in your 11th House of Groups that could lead to a parting of the ways with a colleague or friend.

TUESDAY 1

WEDNESDAY 2 ○

THURSDAY 3

FRIDAY 4

SATURDAY 5 ★ Preparing for an important presentation takes on urgency now

SUNDAY 6 ★

MONDAY 7 ★

TUESDAY 8 ★

WEDNESDAY 9

THURSDAY 10 ★ Enthusiasm allows you to be more open than usual

FRIDAY 11 ★

SATURDAY 12

SUNDAY 13

MONDAY 14

TUESDAY 15

WEDNESDAY 16 ●

THURSDAY 17

FRIDAY 18

SATURDAY 19 ★ Use caution to avoid expensive excesses

SUNDAY 20 ★

MONDAY 21 ★

TUESDAY 22

WEDNESDAY 23

THURSDAY 24 ★ SUPER NOVA DAYS Power struggles are possible

FRIDAY 25 ★

SATURDAY 26 ★

SUNDAY 27 ★

MONDAY 28

TUESDAY 29

WEDNESDAY 30

THURSDAY 31 ○

2010 HOROSCOPE

VIRGO

AUGUST 23–SEPTEMBER 22

OVERVIEW OF THE YEAR

A rare alignment this year among Jupiter, Saturn, Uranus, and Pluto occurs in the houses of your chart associated with values, challenging you to question your core principles in the key areas of finances, self-expression, and intimacy. Saturn spends most of the year in your 2nd House of Resources, focusing your attention on your income. Keeping a steady cash flow would be comforting, yet when confident Jupiter enters fast-moving Aries and your 8th House of Shared Resources on June 6, **opportunities to earn even more can tempt you to sacrifice safety in pursuit of a bigger payoff**. Even if you're normally risk-averse—as Virgos often are—the call for move-ment is so great this year that it will be nearly impossible to resist.

The ways you express yourself in person and through creative activities are due for adjustment now, too. Exacting Pluto's long-term transit through your demonstrative 5th House can force tough choices about how you spend your time and money on January 31 and August 21, when Saturn forms demanding squares. These are uncompromising reminders that you must either work harder for attention or fall back into the shadows of non-recognition. **A Solar Eclipse in this house on January 15 is another sign that it's time to put more effort presenting yourself and your ideas to others**. Training in public speaking or classes in a creative art can help you overcome any shyness or insecurity. Uranus the Awakener forms a supportive sextile to the eclipse that can stimulate unexpected interest in a totally new field; suddenly you're more excited about your life—and more exciting to others. On June 26, a Lunar Eclipse in your 5th House is closely conjunct Pluto and square Jupiter, Saturn, and Uranus. This might provoke a crisis or produce a breakthrough in romantic matters, with children, or in the ways you enjoy yourself. **Still, in this transformational year, it's better to push the envelope and be the agent for change rather than futilely trying to resist it.**

Your ruling planet, Mercury, has four retrograde periods in 2010 that are likely to mess with your plans and require recalculations. The year begins with Mercury retrograde in your 5th House of Love until January 15, creating romantic complications or asking you to put in more practice before a big presentation. Mercury retrograde in your 9th House of Travel and Education from April 18 until May 11 may delay a trip or necessitate makeup work in the classroom. With Mercury retrograde in your 1st House of Self from August 20 until September 12, expect changes of attitude and appearance. And the Messenger's retrograde of December 10–30 starts in your independent 9th House then ends in your 8th House of Deep Sharing. Consider renegotiating as a way to keep relationships healthy.

LOVER'S LEAP

It could be "out with the old and in with the new" this year when it comes to love. Eclipses in your 5th House of Romance on January 15 and June 26 foretell changes in matters of the heart, while Pluto's continuing presence here peels away layers of illusion to reveal deeper underlying desires. Still, generous Jupiter increases opportunities to share your feelings with a worthy person during its visits to your 7th House of Partnerships on January 17–June 6 and September 9–January 22, 2011. You're due for an upgrade in the quality of your amorous experiences, whether by finding someone new with whom to share delight or by reviving the spirit of what originally attracted you to your current partner. Above all, remember that the magic of love isn't something that just happens to you; it's something you can create with intention and a conscious commitment to making it real.

ENOUGH IS ENOUGH

Inspirational Neptune's long transit through your 6th House of Work continues this year, spurring your imagination on the job or wearing you out with self-sacrifice. Neptune joins the New Moon in this house on February 13 to remind you that you're giving too much—or perhaps redirect you toward a more fulfilling job. On June 12, the New Moon in your 10th House of Career and Public Life can push you into the spotlight and increase your professional responsibilities. Spreading your-self too thin remains an issue, so learning how to delegate, rather than doing everything yourself, can be the key to maintaining a position of respect and influence.

BEAR MARKET

The year could start with complications caused by debt or problematic financial partners because Mars, the ruler of your 8th House of Shared Resources, is retrograde until March 10. Avoid new investments, especially highly speculative ones, and don't allow yourself to be bullied in money matters. Cleaning up old obligations should be your first priority. Venus, the ruler of your 2nd House of Income, joins Saturn in this house on August 8, initiating a time of tight fiscal control. Although this could indicate contraction, it also teaches discipline, helping you manage your cash flow more carefully and establish a solid long-term economic plan. Venus is retrograde from October 8 until November 18, indicating the need for a budget adjustment, perhaps due to unexpected expenses.

A HEALTHY FOUNDATION

Pragmatic Saturn is in your 1st House of Physicality from April 7 until July 21, setting the tone for your health and vitality for years to come. Don't try to cut out every last carb and exercise two hours a day—that's not a realistic plan. Working toward modest goals through a safe and simple approach that's well within your reach is sustainable and, therefore, better for you in the long run. If you're doing everything right but still lack energy, ask your health practitioner to check you out for allergies. Mercury's retrograde on August 20 through September 12 occurs in your 1st House, tempting you to drift away from your healthy habits. Don't let discouragement undermine all your good work. This period is only a short break in your routine; you can easily recommence if you don't get overly self-critical.

SHARING IS CARING

Emotional satisfaction comes from good companions, whether you live with them or not. Jupiter, a
ruler of your 4th House of Home and Family, enters
your 7th House of Partnerships on January 17
and remains in relationship houses for the rest
of the year. Those closest to you may have beliefs
very different from your own, yet your ability to
maintain an open dialogue allows you to feel safe
with them anyway. Look to overcome uncertainty
in your domestic life on December 5 when the
optimistic Sagittarius New Moon in your 4th
House forms a stabilizing sextile with Saturn.

SLICE OF HEAVEN

Manifesting your desire to expand your horizons into a true-life experience is possible this year. On May 13, the New Moon in determined Taurus falls in your 9th House of Travel and Education; there it forms harmonious sextiles with adventurous Jupiter and Uranus, sparking an interest in visiting exotic places or studying unusual subjects. Letting your imagination run away with you—not your usual style, Virgo—is perfect right now, since mythical Neptune squares the New Moon to awaken your intuition. And solid Saturn forms a trine that can turn your dream into reality. Unless you're planning a reunion tour, avoid travel from October 8 until November 18 when Venus, the ruler of your 9th House of Faraway Places, will be retrograde.

FALL BACK, SPRING FORWARD

Sometimes you have to fall back a little to prepare yourself for the next great leap forward. Dynamic Mars starts the year moving retrograde in your 12th House of Spirituality. You may sense your connection with the divine slipping away and worry that you're unsupported in your struggle for meaning. Descending into doubt, though, can take you to what feels like the bottom of your soul, from which the only movement is up. Then Mars turns direct in heroic Leo on March 10, rekindling the flame of faith to light your way to a boldly expressive and courageously loving year ahead.

RICK & JEFF'S TIP FOR THE YEAR
Look Outside the Box

Challenges to the core truths you cling to can be a source of irritation and a cause of physical, mental, and emotional fatigue. The battles you face, though, are not with outside forces but within yourself. It's time to reexamine the ideas that have kept your life in order for years, but may be holding you back. What worked in the past won't necessarily be effective now. The desire to return to familiar places in your mind is understandable, but it's not likely to be productive. Certainly, you need times to retreat and take refuge in comfortable concepts. Catch your breath when you can, yet remember: You'll grow much stronger by moving ahead than by turning back.

JANUARY

RAY OF LIGHT

Complete old business before starting new projects with Mercury, your ruling planet, retrograde until **January 15**. This could reduce your efficiency and take the edge off your usually razor-sharp thinking, though it's helpful sometimes to give your brain a break. This retrograde cycle occurs in your 5th House of Love and Play where the emphasis is more on the heart than the head. To succeed at untangling emotional knots and loosening creative blocks, allow your instincts to lead your intellect. Feeling your way through personal situations is a more direct route to the inner truth you seek. Structuring Saturn's retrograde turn on **January 13** is another strong yet subtle signal to search for answers within.

Expect a marked change of direction at the Capricorn New Moon on **January 15**, just as Mercury ends its retrograde cycle. This lunation—a Solar Eclipse in your expressive 5th House—casts light on old relationship matters, revealing where you need to let go and urging you to re-create love with fresh resolve. Stylish Venus conjuncts the eclipse, enticing you to develop your artistic skills and bring more beauty into your life. On **January 17**, giant Jupiter enters compassionate Pisces and your 7th House of Companions, where it stays until **June 6**. You'll encounter generosity from people who expect very little in return. Reaching out to others by sharing your hopes and dreams will inspire them and win you a good deal of support. The dramatic Leo Full Moon on **January 30** is conjunct combative Mars and can expose anger that's been bubbling under the surface. Facing conflict directly may be frightening, but will only make you stronger.

KEEP IN MIND THIS MONTH

Permitting yourself to receive is not only gracious, but also a wonderful way to invite people to share your life more meaningfully.

KEY DATES

SUPER NOVA DAYS

★ **JANUARY 4–5**
word play
Your perception deepens and your words take
on new power when retrograde Mercury joins
the Sun on **January 4**. You can speak with
authority without raising your voice, making
your thoughts crystal clear to others, even
though you're not in the mood to listen to
opposing points of view. Verbal Mercury joins
flirty Venus on **January 5**, prompting sweet
conversations and maybe even talk of love.
Witty repartee is a delight right now—although
expansive Jupiter's semisquare to Mercury
can produce too much verbiage or skew your
judgment with excessive information.

★ **JANUARY 11**
lead with your heart
Strong but sensitive people join your orbit as
the expressive Sun and gracious Venus join
each other and the Moon's North Node in
ambitious Capricorn. Use your charm for a

specific purpose and your chances of success can increase dramatically. Showing your authority with a tender touch is ideal for winning hearts and minds at work and in your private life.

★ **JANUARY 15**
let go and grow
Mercury turns direct, getting you back on track mentally, while the constructive Capricorn New Moon nudges you to be more open in expressing your ambitions. Romance can flourish when you approach it with specific goals in mind, and creative activities take root if you define your intentions carefully. If you're burdened by a frustrating project or immature individuals, however, it's time for drastic changes. Cutting back on your commitment or eliminating someone from the team may be the only way to move forward.

★ **JANUARY 18–19**
try something new
Fresh approaches to your job, colleagues, and daily routine present themselves when Venus

enters your 6th House of Work on **January 18**, followed by the Sun on **January 19**. You may be nudged out of your comfort zone by unconventional individuals or methods you haven't mastered yet. Keeping an open mind will allow you to adjust to unfamiliar conditions, while resisting them will just up the tension.

★ **JANUARY 24–26**
on shaky ground
Facts grow fuzzy when Mercury slides into a semisquare with elusive Neptune on **January 24**. Don't buy a story that sounds too good to be true, even if it's from a reliable source. Imagination is a wonderful thing, but creating your own fantasy is healthier than falling for someone else's. An irritating Venus-Uranus semisquare on **January 25** puts you in a jumpy mood; it's difficult to know where you stand with others. Don't bother defending a position that can change at any moment. Happily, a stroke of genius on **January 26** reveals order in the midst of chaos to make sense out of a crazy situation.

FEBRUARY

SPIRIT OF COOPERATION

Valentine's month could be especially sweet for you this year. The first hint of something magical happening in relationships comes when alluring Venus enters Pisces and your 7th House of Partnerships on **February 11**. If you have someone special in your life, this adds a puff of fairy dust to delightfully inspire your union. If you're single, Venus not only makes you feel more attractive, but also tends to pull kinder people into your world. Although the Aquarius New Moon on **February 13** falls in your 6th House of Work and Service—not the sexiest place in your chart—it, too, is overflowing with inspiration to elevate your spirit and enrich your daily life. Idealistic Neptune and compassionate Chiron join this Sun-Moon conjunction to reveal spiritual meaning and higher purpose that can morph ordinary activities into divine experiences.

The themes of relationship and revelation come together when the Sun enters mystical Pisces and your 7th House on **February 18**. You can now smooth out the rough edges of unsatisfying connections by forgiveness and letting go of little issues that seem to matter less now. Your own spirit of generosity makes it easier to give more to others, be less critical of yourself, and receive more in return. Success in the public arena also comes from greater self-confidence that spurs you to take more creative risks. Demonstrating strength in a relaxed manner makes you a more attractive professional and personal partner. The Full Moon in critical Virgo on **February 28** opposes excessive Jupiter, which could magnify your insecurities or signal enormous potential for growth . . . if you're willing to work hard to make it happen.

KEEP IN MIND THIS MONTH

Don't let minor details distract you from the big picture. When your intentions are on target, the small stuff works itself out.

KEY DATES

★ **FEBRUARY 5–6**
unlikely allies
Gigantic Jupiter lurches from a clumsy
quincunx with Saturn on **February 5** to a slick
sextile with Pluto on **February 6**, turning
an awkward connection with someone into
an effective one. An association that seems
like it can't possibly work can quickly become
rewarding when an ingenious sextile between
Mercury and Uranus shows you how to sidestep power struggles and align your forces in
uniquely productive ways.

★ **FEBRUARY 12–13**
planting seeds
Your thinking is concise and efficient with a
practical Mercury-Saturn trine working on
your behalf on **February 12**. However,
Mercury's opposition to feisty Mars early on
the **13th** hastens thoughts and heats up conversations, perhaps leading to conflict. Still,
the New Moon in cool Aquarius is conjunct the
forgiving planetary duo of Neptune and Chiron,

which helps you find room for competing
points of view. Ideally, dreams seeded by this
New Moon are energetically discussed and
quickly turned into action.

★ **FEBRUARY 16–17**
shared delights
The delicious union of Venus and Jupiter in your
7th House of Relationships on **February 16**
brings you the gifts of good friends, open-
hearted individuals, and generous souls who
magnify your sense of self-worth. It's a good
time to seek support, including funding, for new
ideas. Restless feelings may arise during the
day with an electric Mercury-Uranus semisquare exact later that night. The pace of your
life is bound to pick up, yet if you can apply your
nervous energy with originality, you could see a
breakthrough idea emerge.

★ **FEBRUARY 22–23**
uphill battle
Conversations grow thick as mental Mercury
runs into the ongoing square between Saturn
and Pluto, blocking your repeated attempts to

explain yourself on the job. You might be frustrated by power plays or people who withhold information. Patience is the key now. Slow down and back up your statements with facts if you hope to overcome others' reluctance to believe you.

SUPER NOVA DAYS

★ **FEBRUARY 27–28**
psychic connections
Your intuition is right on target and you are super-sensitive to others when messenger Mercury joins metaphysical Neptune and caring Chiron on **February 27**. You're tapping into higher levels of thought that allow you to comprehend complex concepts and discuss delicate subjects with ease. The healing power of words is a gift you can give and also be open to receive. The Full Moon in your sign on **February 28** opposite beneficent Jupiter attracts wise individuals and open-minded people who recognize your talents in ways you may not. A less critical attitude allows you to speak the truth with a sweet simplicity that makes it easier for others to understand.

MARCH

UPPING THE
RELATIONSHIP ANTE

Shakeups in relationships are a significant issue this month as planets continue to revitalize your 7th House of Partnerships. Mercury, your mentally active ruling planet, enters this house on **March 1**, opening channels of communication and bringing sensitive subjects to the surface. The supernatural Pisces New Moon in your 7th House on **March 15** triggers an explosion of fresh perspectives and surprises that are bound to reshape some of the major connections in your life. With revolutionary Uranus in close conjunction to the Sun, breakdowns and breakthroughs can suddenly cut you loose from people and patterns that no longer suit your needs. Creative discoveries, overactive fantasies, and spiritual pursuits may reawaken your interest in a current partnership or open the door to a new one.

You can touch a new level of commitment as three planets move into your 8th House of Intimacy to test the intensity of your desires and your willingness to push ahead and deepen the connection. The process begins with vivacious Venus entering spontaneous Aries on **March 7**, sparking a frisky attitude as you pursue new pleasures and potential financial rewards. When Mercury follows on **March 17**, you initiate a more direct way of communicating that cuts through your usual reticence and gets straight to the point. While being blunt can provoke arguments, it also brings issues out into the open where you can face your fear of rejection or conflict head-on and learn how to get past it. Opening yourself to new experiences takes you to exciting places when the Sun enters Aries and your 8th House on **March 20**, marking the Spring Equinox. This heralds a new season of engagement as you find greater courage and, perhaps, attract more worthy partners.

KEEP IN MIND THIS MONTH

There's no need to interpret disagreement as failure. In fact, it can be a significant step toward understanding and closeness.

KEY DATES

★ **MARCH 1–2**
temporary meltdown
Mercury's entrance into watery Pisces is supposed to soften communication and take the edge off criticism. However, a stressful quincunx with aggressive Mars on **March 1** and with restrictive Saturn on **March 2** could prove extremely frustrating. You may grow angry if you feel you're being blindsided or challenged by a task for which you're not prepared. Uncooperative individuals may refuse to compromise, so it's up to you to spell out your needs more clearly. Don't expect a response before you've allowed time for serious consideration.

★ **MARCH 7–9**
the things we do for love
New sources of pleasure pop up on **March 7** when Venus enters your 8th House and forms an inviting trine with passionate Mars. An intellectually rich Mercury-Jupiter conjunction opens the floodgates of conversation, and a

73

hopeful attitude makes anything seem possible with the right person. This initial enthusiasm, however, can be stifled on **March 9** when sweet Venus runs into an opposition with stonewalling Saturn. This is the time to build a plan around the excitement you felt and turn that impulse of attraction or a creative idea into something that lasts. The potential rewards are still there; you just have to work extra hard to make them real.

SUPER NOVA DAYS

★ **MARCH 15–18**
question authority
Relationships turn electric on **March 15** when Mercury and unruly Uranus connect with the New Moon, stimulating rapid-fire conversations and sudden changes that can turn your head in every direction. Your feelings about those you're with can change in an instant. This is not a time for commitment but one when strange new ideas about relating are up for consideration. On **March 18**, Mercury opposes conservative Saturn, putting the brakes on this runaway train of possibilities.

★ **MARCH 20–21**

not so innocent

The freshness of the first day of spring is dampened by the skepticism of a Mercury-Pluto square on **March 20**. Serious news, self-doubt, or an abuse of trust forces you to look deeper to understand someone's motivations, perhaps even your own. A complicated opposition between the Sun and Saturn on **March 21** can reinforce this heavy mood. Yet you can use your innate self-discipline and patience to overcome a restrictive authority figure or manage new responsibilities with dignity and self-respect.

★ **MARCH 25**

emotional recycling

A loss turns into a transformational opportunity as the Sun in your 8th House of Deep Sharing squares Pluto in your 5th House of Self-Expression. Don't struggle to hold on to what you have; letting go frees up creative resources that will lead you to something or someone better.

APRIL

SECOND CHANCES

You're sure that you're getting a handle on long-term goals when Mercury enters earthy Taurus and your 9th House of Future Vision on **April 2**, yet it's wise to consider any current plan as a rough draft. That's because rational Mercury makes a U-turn and goes retrograde on **April 18**, starting three weeks of review and revision that can alter your aspirations or the way you intend to reach them. Travel and education are particularly susceptible to last-minute changes. Responsible Saturn is already retrograde, but its reentry into Virgo on **April 7**—where it stays until **July 21**—is another signal that you may have to retreat and reorganize before you can advance. Don't despair if you find yourself addressing personal problems you thought were behind you. Saturn's final visit to your sign enables you to become even more successful in dealing with unresolved issues.

Sparks fly with the New Moon in impetuous Aries on **April 14** in your 8th House of Intimacy and Shared Resources. Don't allow yourself to be rushed into a commitment by an impatient indi-vidual. New personal and financial connections are possible, yet with retrograde Mercury coming up it's best to look twice before jumping in. On **April 26**, rigid Saturn opposes eccentric Uranus for the fourth time before a final occurrence on **July 26**. Conflict between your need for order and the unpredictability of others reminds you that you can't control every outside event. The Full Moon in sultry Scorpio on **April 28** spurs intense conversations in your 3rd House of Communication. Revealing secrets will have powerful consequences, so be discreet about the information you choose to share.

KEEP IN MIND THIS MONTH

The slower you, go the farther you'll get. A more deliberate approach will radically reduce the mistakes that would otherwise cost you time and energy.

KEY DATES

★ **APRIL 4–6**
cool hand Luke
Talking too much or too fast can incite an
argument when chatty Mercury forms an
overblown semisquare with Jupiter on **April 4**
and a tense square with Mars on **April 5**. You
can end up looking very strong if you maintain
your cool in the face of information overload or
an angry individual. Mercury's creative trine
with surgical Pluto on **April 6** helps you cut
through clutter, get to the heart of the matter,
and communicate with conviction.

★ **APRIL 10–11**
sixth sense
You may feel frustrated beyond reason by outside pressures now. Fortunately, Mercury's
brilliant quintile with imaginative Neptune on
April 10 shows you ways to work around the
thorniest obstacles. Avoid using force and
your intuition should reveal a subtle means of
reducing tension. On **April 11**, a Venus-Uranus
semisquare invites you to loosen up and

experiment with new forms of pleasure and enjoying yourself with others.

SUPER NOVA DAYS

★ **APRIL 17–18**
delicious distractions
Passion rules on **April 17**: Venus in sensual Taurus starts the day with a tense aspect to emotionally extreme Pluto and finishes it with a sweet sextile to generous Jupiter. What begins with doubt and isolation should end with a rush of joy. Besides, it's time to set aside analysis, calculations, and worry. Your ruling planet, Mercury, comes to a dead stop on **April 18**, a reminder to pause and rest your mind before the onrush of obligations refills your head with a million and one things to do.

★ **APRIL 23–24**
temporary insecurity
You may be feeling self-conscious on **April 23** with the Moon in your sign and approval-hungry Venus made vulnerable by a square with supersensitive Neptune. It's easy now to overreact to criticism or to lose yourself in

romantic fantasy. Relief comes quickly, though: A Venus-Uranus sextile attracts you to unusual people or experiences that help you shake off a sense of uncertainty. Solid ground in your social life is evident on **April 24** when a Venus-Saturn trine helps you regain trust in others—and in yourself.

★ **APRIL 28**
metaphysical mirror
The Scorpio Full Moon occurs in your 3rd House of Communication as retrograde Mercury joins the Sun, a combination rich in its potential for enhancing your self-aware-ness. Your new insight may reveal desires and fears that weren't obvious before. If you feel afraid or angry, remember that today is more about uncovering an inconvenient truth about yourself than whatever anyone else is saying.

MAY

WIDE, WIDE WORLD

Reshaping a long-range vision to fit your current reality can turn this into a highly productive month for you. Adjusting your sights is easier when sharp-eyed Mercury turns direct in your 9th House of Big Ideas on **May 11**. The maintenance work of the three previous weeks pays off with a clearer path to the journey of your dreams, additional education, or a philosophical awakening. The sensible Taurus New Moon in your 9th House on **May 13** underscores the opportunities that come from casting your mind beyond the limits of your daily routine and seeing yourself in a wider world of meaning and purpose. Harsh squares to the New Moon from restless Mars and boundless Neptune may produce unreachable fantasies and irritating challenges. Yet even the wildest of dreams may come true as concrete Saturn and visionary Jupiter support this lunation. Let inspiration take you as far as it can, then allow those images to sink in deeply before you act on them.

The Sun's entry into jittery Gemini and your 10th House of Public Responsibility on **May 20** could lead to overcommitment and too many distractions. However, Jupiter's opposition to practical Saturn on **May 23**—which recurs on **August 16** and **January 4, 2011**—pulls you back to a more strategic perspective that helps you set priorities. Scintillating Uranus enters excitable Aries and your 8th House of Intimacy on **May 27**— staying there until **August 13** and then settling in for a seven-year stay on **March 11, 2011**—to enliven partnerships with surprises. The fiery Full Moon in far-reaching Sagittarius on **May 27** feeds your 4th House of Security with a taste for adventure that encourages honesty and risk taking, both at home and in your professional life.

KEEP IN MIND THIS MONTH

Your excitement about a brighter future needs to be turned down to a low simmer so you can cook up the sauce of success at a manageable pace.

KEY DATES

SUPER NOVA DAYS

★ **MAY 2–4**
playing detective

Saturn and Neptune form a slippery quincunx on **May 2** that can wear you out if you don't handle your workload carefully. A series of hard aspects on **May 3 and May 4** builds tension, especially with authority figures.

Unmovable individuals can provoke your anger, leading to a sudden explosion. Still, the deep thinking of an insightful Mercury-Pluto trine on the **3rd** can reveal to you the underlying issues and help you resolve matters with precise words and deeds.

★ **MAY 9–11**
don't speak

Discretion is essential on **May 9**—a day when careless comments can incite strong emotions. Avoid quick responses to pushy people on **May 11**, because Mercury's direct turn punishes spontaneity and rewards careful reflection.

★ **MAY 17–18**
bumpy road ahead
High expectations can get cut down to size as desirous Venus whets your appetite for pleasure with a square to extravagant Jupiter on **May 17**, followed by a square with naysayer Saturn on **May 18**. This abrupt shift from insatiable hunger for love, pleasure, and approval to a steel curtain of denial can be confusing for relationships—both personal and professional. It may be hard to trust others or your own judgment. A tough Mars-Pluto sesquisquare on the **17th** can bring frustration to a boil; happily, a more forgiving mood arrives with a Venus-Neptune trine late the following day.

★ **MAY 23**
make love, not war
It won't take much to arouse deep feelings today, for an intense opposition between passionate Venus and manipulative Pluto occurs on the same day as the Jupiter-Saturn opposition. This pair of 180-degree angles can whip you through highs and lows of hope and doubt

that stir up buried feelings of resentment or regret. Still, getting to the heart of what you hunger for can energize you. You're motivated now to make profound changes in how you use your talents to attract the love and money you desire.

★ **MAY 27–29**
conceptual blueprints
Family secrets may be revealed in an outburst of honesty fueled by the blunt Sagittarius Full Moon in your 4th House of Roots on **May 27**. You could feel overwhelmed by the truth and unprepared to use it effectively. Talkative Mercury's tense aspects to Saturn on **May 28** and Jupiter on **May 29** give your words extra weight. Instead of letting them be held against you, fix them in your mind to shape your vision for the future. It's essential to counter any negative thinking with constructive ideas to keep the doors of opportunity open wide.

JUNE

COUNTING ON CHANGE

Major opportunities can come and go in a flash, so be ready to grab the brass ring while you can. Bountiful Jupiter gets the ball rolling by entering rash Aries and your 8th House of Shared Resources on **June 6**. There it will spend the next three months urging you to keep pace with the movers and shakers of the world. Normally, you prefer to manage your life more carefully, especially with Mars entering methodical Virgo on **June 7**. The action planet's presence in your sign boosts your energy, but be careful not to squander it defending what you already have; taking the initiative to start new projects is more rewarding. Jupiter joins revolutionary Uranus on **June 8** in the first of three awakenings that recur on **September 18** and **January 4, 2011**. Jumping into or out of a business or personal partnership is risky, yet it's better than distracting yourself with petty details while a big chance slips away.

The New Moon in versatile Gemini on **June 12** seeds your 10th House of Career with new ideas and responsibilities that can pile up in the weeks ahead. You must reduce your obligations now as the tidal wave of change continues to rise. The Sun's entry into defensive Cancer on **June 21**—the Summer Solstice—is preceded by a square to Saturn on the **19th** and followed by squares to Uranus the **21st** and Jupiter on the **23rd**. These intense aspects pull, inspire, and tire you out with an overload of challenges and chores. Finally, on **June 26**, the ambitious Capricorn Full Moon Eclipse conjuncts transformational Pluto, eliminating the old to make way for the new.

KEEP IN MIND THIS MONTH

Putting others first can work for a while, but will wear you out if you continue to ignore your own needs to serve theirs.

KEY DATES

★ **JUNE 3-4**
chasing ghosts
Strong opinions don't necessarily lead to
effective action when a mentally intense
sesquisquare between Mercury and Pluto on
June 3 is followed by a spacey Mars-Neptune
opposition on **June 4**. The first pair can draw
you into an argument or narrow your thinking.
Concentration is useful, of course, but not
when it leads to obsession over a detail that
blocks your view of the big picture. The upside
of spiritual Neptune's opposition to energetic
Mars is the ability to act with great tenderness
and imagination. Just remember how much
effort you can waste pursuing fantasies or
fighting for lost causes.

★ **JUNE 9-11**
clever solutions
Take some time out to dream on **June 9** when
a Mercury-Neptune square fuzzes facts and
confuses conversations, but also opens
your mind to a world of fantasy. Creativity,

especially related to your career, is kicked up another notch on **June 10** when Mercury enters curious Gemini and forms brilliant sextiles to Jupiter and Uranus. You can sell new ideas with a combination of originality and enthusiasm that's hard for others to resist. To resolve sticky problems quickly, look beyond the rulebook to come up with your own answers. Discussions, though, can grow heated with a fierce Mercury-Mars square on **June 11** that puts passion before reason.

★ **JUNE 16–17**
stroke of genius
In a month rich with bright ideas, this could be the most creative time of all. Mercury's innovative quintiles with Jupiter and Uranus reveal previously unforeseen combinations of information that blast open your awareness. Describing what you see to others, though, can be difficult, especially if they lack imagination. Simplify your ideas, if you can, or wait for a better time to get your point across.

SUPER NOVA DAYS

★ **JUNE 24–28**
choose a side
You can work through a tense issue about
authority and control on **June 24** by realizing
that it isn't the matter of principle it seems to
be. Besides, it may all be water under the
bridge when Mercury moves into caring Cancer
on **June 25** and forms a square with unstable
Uranus. Nervousness and uncertainty are
hanging in the air; you may be sensing a profound change coming that's signaled by an
opposition between the Sun and Pluto on the
25th plus the Full Moon Eclipse on the **26th**. A
power struggle could arise, but the real issue
is for you to learn where to let go and where to
invest yourself more deeply. Debate continues
as Mercury squares opinionated Jupiter and
opposes Pluto on **June 26–27**. Clarity finally
arrives when Mercury joins the Sun on **June 28**,
aligning intellect and intention to set your
direction more firmly.

JULY

HEART RULES HEAD

Thinking gives way to feeling for much of this month, Virgo. Cerebral Mercury slips into your 12th House of Escapism on **July 9**, followed by sensual Venus's entry into Virgo on **July 10**. Giving your brain a break to focus on personal matters, including your appearance, allows you to have a good time without worrying quite so much about the million and one details that usually occupy your mind. The New Moon on **July 11** is a Solar Eclipse in emotional Cancer and your 11th House of Groups and Friends. Finding a comfortable place on a team or among your pals may involve changing your role or approach. Productive Mars in Virgo sextiles this eclipse, motivating you to cut out who and what you no longer need and increasing your effectiveness working or playing with others.

Saturn reenters objective Libra on **July 21**, returning your attention to economic matters during its two-year stay in your 2nd House of Resources. Be persistent as you renegotiate financial partnerships when prosperous Jupiter turns retrograde on **July 23** and squares purging

Pluto on **July 25**. Intimacy issues may also be agitated as secrets come to light. The Aquarius Full Moon on **July 25** lands in your 6th House of Employment and is supported by Saturn and Uranus, helping you establish new skills or perhaps even shift to a different line of work. Saturn's final opposition to rebellious Uranus on **July 26** could mark the end of a long struggle in relationships as you realize that being true to yourself is the only way to feel free. Your ability to state your needs clearly is enhanced when Mercury enters matter-of-fact Virgo on **July 27**.

KEEP IN MIND THIS MONTH

Your emotional intelligence grows when you listen to your gut instincts rather than rationalizing away feelings that don't fit your preconceived notions.

KEY DATES

★ **JULY 1–3**
twisted logic
Getting straight answers from others or making yourself understood can be tricky on **July 1** when logical Mercury is muddled by squishy Neptune. While words may flow like poetry, details can get lost in the mix. On **July 3**, however, a clever quintile between Mercury and well-organized Saturn restores intellectual order and gets communication back on track.

★ **JULY 10–11**
you are so beautiful
Magnetic Venus enters your 1st House of Personality on **July 10**, increasing your sense of self-worth. Instead of focusing on your flaws, commit to improving what you can change and accepting what you can't. The more you like yourself, the more appealing you'll be to others. You could have so many creative ideas on **July 11** that you have to let some of them go. A difference of opinion may get out of hand, so if you find tension

building, gracefully back out before any real
damage is done.

★ **JULY 17–19**
grinding gears
Mercury forms hard aspects with Saturn on
July 17, Uranus on **July 18**, plus Jupiter and
Pluto on the **19th**, sending you through a mill
of mood changes. Saturn hands you doubt and
resistance, forcing you to slow down and prove
yourself. Uranus supplies surprises, destabi-
lizing you with uncertainty yet, perhaps,
opening your eyes to untested ideas. Jupiter
drops off an overload of data and tasks that
ruthless Pluto requires you to cut down to a
manageable size.

SUPER NOVA DAYS

★ **JULY 25–27**
system upgrade
The Aquarius Full Moon on **July 25** shines
attention on your daily routine. Work, health,
and your regular practices are ripe for renova-
tion. Wise Saturn's supportive trine to the Full
Moon provides a solid framework for changing

habits in a responsible way. You may find yourself distracted on **July 26**, when Mercury opposes Neptune, but you can compensate when the messenger planet enters its earthy home sign Virgo on **July 27**. Sharp thinking helps you discern where to let go of the old and commit to the new as Saturn and Uranus make their final opposition on the **26th**.

★ **JULY 30–31**
crisis management
Motivating Mars is firing through your 2nd House of Resources, pushing you to seek new ways to earn money and increase your assets. His alignment with volatile Uranus and crystallizing Saturn forces you to quickly take a stand in response to unexpected events. You need to gain control of the situation as fast as possible. If you catch a whiff of an exciting opportunity, take concrete action right away to make sure it lasts.

AUGUST

FINISH TO START

This transitional month finds you looking back over the past to decide where to reinvest your energy in old projects and relationships, and where you must bid a fond farewell and move on. With the Sun in your 12th House of Endings until **August 23**, it's a great time to clean out your emotional and physical closets. Retreating from the world creates a quiet space in which you reaffirm your connection with faith, nature, and the divine to fuel imagination and turn dreams into reality. Wise Jupiter's square to transformational Pluto on **August 3** also exposes the cost of desire, helping you decide where to hang on and where to let go. The Leo New Moon on **August 9** plants seeds of creative magic in your spiritual 12th House, encouraging boldness and boosting your confidence.

You may see advances delayed in August while your ruling planet, Mercury, slows down prior to turning retrograde in your sign on **August 20**. You may have to redo recent tasks during the subsequent three weeks, so operate with caution to eliminate errors and reduce redundancy.

Retrograde Jupiter's opposition to oppressive Saturn on **August 16** is another yellow flag, especially in personal and business partnerships. Don't be pushed into premature commitments. The incredibly heavy square of Saturn and Pluto returns for the final time on **August 21**, locking in major decisions for a long-term run. If you have any doubts, just say no. Besides, the intuitive Pisces Full Moon on **August 24** in your 7th House of Relationships brings revelations about a person close to you and may even open the door to meeting someone new.

KEEP IN MIND THIS MONTH

Taking time away from your primary responsibilities gives your brain a rest and lets your imagination flow freely.

KEY DATES

★ **AUGUST 3–4**
anger management
Practicing diplomacy is essential now while self-righteous Jupiter squares off with powerful Pluto on the **3rd** and militant Mars struggles with both Jupiter and Pluto on the **4th**. Although it can be difficult to make compromises under such pressure-packed circumstances, keeping your cool is key to avoiding conflict at work. Self-discipline and a well-designed plan can empower you to promote your interests. Do your homework before trying to establish a strategic alliance with an influential person.

SUPER NOVA DAYS

★ **AUGUST 7–10**
voracious appetite
Manage your expenses carefully on **August 7**, when indulgent Venus in your 2nd House of Money opposes reckless Uranus. Spending carelessly or loving foolishly can prove costly when Venus and the Sun aspect responsible Saturn on **August 8–9**. Still, you may have a

hard time maintaining fiscal discipline or emotional self-control as subjective Venus opposes excessive Jupiter on **August 9** and squares obsessive Pluto on the **10th**. Watch out for extreme reactions—interpreting a minor criticism as a major attack, for instance, or allowing a simple need to grow into an insatiable desire.

★ **AUGUST 16**
careful consideration
The second of three oppositions between Jupiter and Saturn could be a watershed moment with respect to your long-term goals and aspirations. Don't be shy about asking tough questions if you need more information to make an important decision. Doing additional research to find the facts you need ensures that you're making a well-informed choice. Deciding how you best use your resources should not be done in haste.

★ **AUGUST 20**
summer holiday
Overconfidence—whether your own or someone else's—is a warning sign on **August 20** as

the authoritative Sun opposes delusional Neptune. A sexy Venus-Mars conjunction adds to your desire to have fun, even if it means falling for fairy tales. Your brain may be going on vacation since Mercury is currently standing still just before turning retrograde—perfect conditions for play and romance, but risky for commitments. As long as you don't engage in serious business, you can have a great time.

★ **AUGUST 23**
solar power
The Sun enters your sign, kicking you into a higher gear energetically and offering you greater willingness to express yourself. It's wise to apply this increase in confidence to personal matters, where your ability to address your own needs and work with others one-to-one really matters. Complex systems, like those at work, can't be charmed or easily conquered. Mercury is retrograde in your sign, so tighten up your own game before tackling any major challenges. Taking small steps to improve your health and vitality, as well as your self-image, is a wise investment now.

SEPTEMBER

FREE YOUR MIND

The ball is in your court this month as the Virgo New Moon on **September 8** energizes your 1st House of Personality. Taking the initiative is even easier when Mercury turns direct in your sign on **September 12**. This double dose of planetary activity is ideal for kicking off a self-improvement project. Adjusting your diet, altering your appearance, and changing the ways you interact with others work best when you are prepared and well informed about your methods. As always, it's vital to be gentle with yourself, rather than pushing yourself too hard or too fast to achieve your desired goals.

Relationship issues are revived on **September 9** when Jupiter backs into sensitive Pisces and your 7th House of Partnerships, where it stays until **January 22, 2011**; unresolved problems can return in a more dramatic form than before. Emotional excess makes it hard for you to deal with matters rationally, especially when Jupiter joins incendiary Uranus on **September 18**. Still, this aspect raises the possibility of a breakthrough—some kind of radical solution or sudden awakening that frees you from the box of habitual reactions to put the past behind you. If you're single, a meeting with an unusual person can provoke surprising reactions. This could be the igniting spark of a meaningful personal connection or a new professional relationship. Either way, it's best to consider this a time to experiment, rather than one for building a permanent alliance. Clarity about the long-term prospects of any new union will follow the third and final Jupiter-Uranus conjunction on **January 4, 2011**; you'll then know if it has potential to last.

KEEP IN MIND THIS MONTH

Since you can't control the behavior of others— who may be acting irrationally—focus on managing your own life as best you can.

KEY DATES

★ **SEPTEMBER 3–5**
peaceful coexistence
Choose your words carefully and take what others say less personally, because you're acutely sensitive to language right now. Chatty Mercury joins the Sun on **September 3**, increasing self-consciousness, while semi-squares to vulnerable Venus make for delicate conversations. There could be magic on **September 4** when Venus trines Neptune, inspiring creativity and romance, yet tension between Mercury and impatient Mars on **September 5** can quickly take the bloom off the rose if it gives rise to competitive feelings.

★ **SEPTEMBER 8**
new year's resolutions
The annual New Moon in your sign is always a milestone event, one that sows seeds of inten-tion for your year ahead. This Sun-Moon con-junction is close to an awkward semisquare with Venus in passionate Scorpio, reflecting the contrast between your practical aspirations and

your emotional desires. Accepting that both are important allows you to move from duty to delight and back again without judging yourself so harshly that you aren't satisfied with either.

SUPER NOVA DAYS

★ **SEPTEMBER 12-13**
anything goes
Mercury's direct turn on **September 12** coincides with a smoldering Venus-Pluto sextile, encouraging sexy conversations and resourceful thinking. Even if you don't have eroticism on your mind, you're likely to communicate with intensity and frankness. You can also be risky and frisky on **September 13** when Mars skids off quincunxes with the volcanic Jupiter-Uranus conjunction. Cutting yourself enough slack to make mistakes in unfamiliar territory is healthier than trying to maintain order while everyone else is breaking the rules.

★ **SEPTEMBER 21-22**
balancing chaos
You could be in for a wild ride when the Sun in your 1st House of Self opposes Jupiter and

Uranus in your 7th House of Others on **September 21**. Overly enthusiastic individuals can drive you crazy with their unpredictability or excite you with their originality and vision. Either way, you may feel like things are out of control. On **September 22**, the Sun's entry into peacemaking Libra—the Fall Equinox—eases the pressure. You become more comfortable in your own skin and less concerned with the behavior of others.

★ **SEPTEMBER 30**
fiscal discipline
Money matters are on your mind when the Sun joins sobering Saturn in your 2nd House of Resources. If you're encountering limits, the good news is that you have a very clear picture of where you stand and what you need to do to get your financial house in order. Investing in tools or training to increase your income potential is a smart move. A friend or colleague may offer good advice and emotional support to encourage your ambitions.

OCTOBER

SWEET AND SOUR

A shift toward polite and peaceful interactions
appears to get the month off to a pleasant start
when Mercury enters gracious Libra on **October 3**.
Yet the communication planet's tense square with
shadowy Pluto on **October 5** darkens discussions
and could turn your mind in a less trusting direction. The contrast between Libra's happy talk and
a more somber perspective flows in and out
throughout the month. For example, the New
Moon in friendly Libra on **October 7** is normally a
time of romantic innocence and naive optimism.
However, constraining Saturn's close proximity to
Mercury and the Sun-Moon conjunction leaves
you doubting your self-worth and wondering if
you're being treated fairly. Be patient if the potential rewards of the New Moon in your 2nd House
of Income are delayed. Still, investing in develop-
ing your talents and professional skills now will
likely pay off down the road.

A reassessment of resources is on deck for you
with value-driven Venus's retrograde turn on
October 8, which starts in your 3rd House of
Communication and finishes on **November 18** in

your financial 2nd House. Intense discussions and reflection on the past may touch old wounds and, ideally, release their toxic effects. Mercury plunges into Scorpio and your 3rd House on **October 20**, deepening your perceptions and intensifying your words. The irrepressible Aries Full Moon ignites your 8th House of Intimacy on **October 22**, pushing a personal or professional partnership to the brink. The Sun's entry into insightful Scorpio on **October 23** can seal the deal as you consciously express your willingness to go farther—or recognize that you've reached the end of the road and need to turn in a new direction.

KEEP IN MIND THIS MONTH

The opinions you form and statements you make can have lasting power. Reflect carefully and kindly before sending them out into orbit.

KEY DATES

★ **OCTOBER 1–2**
technicolor fantasies
Your imagination is uncharacteristically vivid on **October 1** when Mercury shifts from a quincunx with dreamy Neptune to an opposition with optimistic Jupiter. These aspects are better for creative fiction than hard cold facts, so speak with a smile to show you're just kidding, and take what you hear with a grain of salt. Electricity is in the air with kinetic Uranus opposing Mercury on **October 2**. This pair brings originality along with erratic thinking, provoking impulsive words and actions.

★ **OCTOBER 8**
the sounds of silence
It's time to be thoughtful with messenger Mercury joining solemn Saturn while Venus turns retrograde. Your every word is weighted with extra meaning, even when you're trying to be light and playful. This is excellent for serious talk about personal matters, yet makes it difficult to relax. Confidentiality is crucial and,

in fact, "no comment" could be your best response to a delicate question.

SUPER NOVA DAYS

★ **OCTOBER 16–18**
ready, aim, readjust
On **October 16**, Mercury joins the Sun, making it easy for you to speak from the heart. This alignment of intellect and identity sharpens your self-awareness and shows you clearly how to manage a job. Yet the edges of your mind soften on **October 17** when lavish Jupiter skews your perceptions with a quincunx to mental Mercury. While this is fine for telling stories, avoid making serious judgments. A balance between the real and the ideal is present on **October 18** with a Mercury-Neptune trine that can support dreams and heal misunderstandings.

★ **OCTOBER 20–22**
defensive driving
Mercury's dive into ruminating Scorpio arrives with an energizing Mars-Jupiter trine on **October 20**. You turn your ideas into action

easily now, especially with the help of generous partners and encouraging allies. You may run into resistance on **October 21** when Mars's forward march is slowed by authoritative Saturn. Don't force issues or allow someone else to set your pace. A Mars-Neptune square on **October 22** can be like hitting an icy patch in the road. Taking your foot off the gas is the best way to protect yourself.

★ **OCTOBER 25–26**
subtle powers of persuasion
Language is a tool for seduction when Mercury joins sexy Venus on **October 25**. The tone and tempo of words are more important now than their literal meaning. Don't allow facts to get in the way of the feelings that tell the real story, and don't overlook the power of eye contact. The atmosphere lightens on **October 26**, yet be careful about growing too cavalier with your commitments. Optimism is a wonderful quality . . . but not when it encourages you to promise more than you should.

NOVEMBER

KIND CANDOR

Honesty is always a virtue, but when and how you express it can make all the difference this month. You start off with your usual high degree of discretion as the Sun, Mercury, and Venus in confidential Scorpio meet in your 3rd House of Communication. The New Moon in this secretive sign on **November 6** may reveal a mystery when someone shares a very private story. Anything you say at a time like this will be taken very seriously when a person who trusts you is this vulnerable. Valuable Venus slips back into her airy home sign Libra on **November 7**, inviting you to reexamine resources in your 2nd House of Money. Adjusting a financial agreement may be necessary before Venus turns forward again on **November 18**.

Expressive Mercury enters outgoing Sagittarius and your 4th House of Roots on **November 8**. You may talk more openly about yourself, even in ways that might normally be embarrassing. It is appropriate, though, to delve into your personal history, recognize how seemingly separate pieces are connected, and conceive a new sense of meaning and purpose. Still, exposing private information about family members and close friends may not be appreciated. Expansive Jupiter turns direct on **November 18**, along with vulnerable Venus, to add to the rising wave of openness. The persevering Taurus Full Moon on **November 21** in your 9th House of Higher Truth continues the trend of speaking out and seeking answers without being cautious or coy. Then, on **November 22**, the Sun moves into Sagittarius and your 4th House. There it shines a bright light of hope, burning away petty issues of the past and opening your eyes to a more inspirational view of the future.

KEEP IN MIND THIS MONTH

Wild leaps will likely miss the mark. Enthusiasm works best when you break it down into small steps toward your goals.

KEY DATES

SUPER NOVA DAYS

★ **NOVEMBER 4–6**
braving the elements
Finding the right balance between unbridled hope and disillusionment makes this a complex and challenging time. On **November 4**, a wide-eyed Mercury-Jupiter trine is so positive that you can easily see how to turn a loss into a gain. This perspective makes you an avid learner and a convincing speaker. Yet on **November 6**, Mercury slides into a square with ungrounded Neptune and bumps into the hard corner of stern Saturn. If you're foggy with the details, the fierce Scorpio New Moon will hold you accountable. Even reliable individuals may let you down. Happily, an ingenious Mercury-Uranus trine can save the day with an unexpected solution.

★ **NOVEMBER 15**
unlimited partnership potential
Hook up with a helpful partner and you can get several days of work done in one. A smart

sextile between dynamic Mars and hardworking Saturn is super-efficient and makes tough
tasks easy. Yet fun does not have to be left out
of the equation. A fat trine between the Sun
and jolly Jupiter in your 7th House of Others
allows you to connect deeply with someone
who shares your sense of humor. Nothing
seems out of reach when you have the right
person on your side.

★ **NOVEMBER 20**
climbing the walls
Sharp thinking and even sharper words are
likely thanks to a high-intensity conjunction of
Mercury and contentious Mars. This union in
your 4th House of Home and Family can provoke a fight in your household. The truth is
that you're restless, so instead of arguing, plan
a vacation or a remodeling project to fulfill
your need for action.

★ **NOVEMBER 25–27**
uncommon combinations
Helping a friend or colleague on **November 25**
may be more complicated than you think. A

small task can turn into a major project, so measure the situation in detail before jumping in. Your creativity is flowing fiercely on **November 27**, though, when Mercury connects with imaginative Neptune and innovative Uranus. You're now able to mesh ideas and activities that have almost nothing in common—Mercury's clever quintile with Saturn shows you how to stitch them together.

★ **NOVEMBER 29–30**
reality rules
You leave behind your fantasies about others when Venus returns to scrutinizing Scorpio and your perceptive 3rd House on **November 29**. Your tendency to demand clarity about your expectations of the people close to you is reinforced as your key planet, Mercury, enters no-nonsense Capricorn on **November 30**. Your patience for schemers and dreamers is reaching an end that may well lead to someone's exit. Still, this is a time when you grow by letting go. Individuals and concepts that can't be made real in the short term may not get to hang around with you for very long.

123

DECEMBER

MAKING YOUR LIST AND CHECKING IT TWICE

The real gifts of the holidays, Virgo, may not arrive for you until the very end of the year, because your ruling planet, Mercury, is retrograde **December 10–30**. Life still advances during this planet's backward cycle, yet you may be more involved with finishing off the old than stepping into the new. Tying up loose ends—especially related to home, family, and creative projects—can keep you from looking ahead until the New Year's ball is about to drop. Seeds for new adventures are planted with the Sagittarius New Moon in your 4th House of Roots on **December 5**. Clear your garden to give them room to germinate and grow. This joyous season is a mix of work and play with active Mars entering disciplined Capricorn in your 5th House of Fun and Games on **December 7**. Don't be surprised if you're asked to organize holiday parties at the office or for your kid's school.

Stormy conditions are brewing at work and at home with a hyperactive Lunar Eclipse on **December 21**. This Full Moon is shaky in the last degree of Gemini, with uncertainty stoked by volatile squares from Jupiter and Uranus. It's easy to be all over the map emotionally now, as both internal feelings and external conditions shift in the blink of an eye. Blowing off steam is helpful as long as it doesn't lead to a breakdown. The Sun's entry into ambitious Capricorn later that day is the Winter Solstice, marking a collective seasonal turn and a renewed personal commitment to a more creative time ahead. The mental train to take you there arrives at the station on **December 30**, ready to thrill you with a fresh start for the New Year.

KEEP IN MIND THIS MONTH

The spirit of the season can be lost without time to relax. Allowing yourself flaws that leave room to breathe is healthier than stifling yourself by demanding perfection.

KEY DATES

★ **DECEMBER 3–5**
suspicious minds
A simple conversation can turn into an explosive event when an agitated Mars-Uranus square on **December 3** undermines compromise and cooperation. However, if you have an original idea, rather than a rebellious attitude, you just might find a way to make it work. Pressure remains on **December 5** with a suspicious Mercury-Pluto conjunction that charges words with extra power. You may be provoking others with probing questions, or you could be on the receiving end of a grilling. Either way, trust and sensitivity will deepen a connection while jealousy or carelessness can harm it.

★ **DECEMBER 10**
savor the moment
Mercury's retrograde turn has the magic of an old-time romance as it forms a sweet sextile with bewitching Venus. Time stands still to reveal beauty where you don't expect it or to

soothe you with loving words of encouragement. Don't rush a conversation just because it's not obviously productive. Pleasure is a valuable commodity that grows if you allow the time and space to indulge in it.

★ **DECEMBER 13**
hot knife through butter
Edges are razor-sharp with a rare triple conjunction of Mercury, Mars, and Pluto. Words can cut someone to the quick—or slice through fuzziness and fakery to get down to bare essentials. You may be dealing with hypersensitive people, so don't push so hard to drive your point home. If you're getting irrational resistance or encountering someone overly aggressive, it may be wise to postpone discussion until common sense returns.

SUPER NOVA DAYS

★ **DECEMBER 19–21**
into the future
Your eyes narrow with concentration as mental Mercury joins the Sun on **December 19**. It can seem like you are peering into the depths of

your soul where truths about your identity are lurking. Flashes of an alternative reality are sparked by a Mercury-Uranus square on **December 20**, blowing off old ideas to prepare for the blastoff of the Lunar Eclipse and Winter Solstice on **December 21**. You could be flooded by information you can't assimilate. Don't try to make sense of all of it now; you're crossing a threshold that can alter your future. Allow time to see where it's taking you.

★ **DECEMBER 29–30**
pace yourself
Managing your financial and physical resources wisely reduces frustration and wasted time when Mars squares frugal Saturn on **December 29**. Slow-and-sure is much more productive than rushing and then waiting impatiently. Mercury's direct turn on **December 30** releases you from the dungeon of redundancy. You can forge ahead freely now that you've taken care of business.

APPENDIXES

★

2010 MONTH-AT-A-GLANCE ASTROCALENDAR

★

FAMOUS VIRGOS

★

VIRGO IN LOVE

FRIDAY 1	
SATURDAY 2	
SUNDAY 3	
MONDAY 4 ★ **SUPER NOVA DAYS** Witty repartee is a delight now	
TUESDAY 5 ★	
WEDNESDAY 6	
THURSDAY 7	
FRIDAY 8	
SATURDAY 9	
SUNDAY 10	
MONDAY 11 ★ Strong but sensitive people join your orbit	
TUESDAY 12	
WEDNESDAY 13	
THURSDAY 14	
FRIDAY 15 ★ ● Creative activities take root if you define your intentions	
SATURDAY 16	
SUNDAY 17	
MONDAY 18 ★ Keeping an open mind allows you to adjust to unusual conditions	
TUESDAY 19 ★	
WEDNESDAY 20	
THURSDAY 21	
FRIDAY 22	
SATURDAY 23	
SUNDAY 24 ★ Don't buy a story that sounds too good to be true	
MONDAY 25 ★	
TUESDAY 26 ★	
WEDNESDAY 27	
THURSDAY 28	
FRIDAY 29	
SATURDAY 30 ○	
SUNDAY 31	

★ designates key date

MONDAY 1

TUESDAY 2

WEDNESDAY 3

THURSDAY 4

FRIDAY 5 ★ Sidestep power struggles now

SATURDAY 6 ★

SUNDAY 7

MONDAY 8

TUESDAY 9

WEDNESDAY 10

THURSDAY 11

FRIDAY 12 ★ Your thinking is concise and efficient

SATURDAY 13 ★ ●

SUNDAY 14

MONDAY 15

TUESDAY 16 ★ Seek support, including funding, for new ideas

WEDNESDAY 17 ★

THURSDAY 18

FRIDAY 19

SATURDAY 20

SUNDAY 21

MONDAY 22 ★ Patience is the key now

TUESDAY 23 ★

WEDNESDAY 24

THURSDAY 25

FRIDAY 26

SATURDAY 27 ★ SUPER NOVA DAYS Your intuition is right on target

SUNDAY 28 ★ ○

MONDAY 1 ★ Uncooperative individuals may refuse to compromise

---

TUESDAY 2 ★

WEDNESDAY 3

THURSDAY 4

FRIDAY 5

SATURDAY 6

SUNDAY 7 ★ New sources of pleasure pop up

MONDAY 8 ★

TUESDAY 9 ★

WEDNESDAY 10

THURSDAY 11

FRIDAY 12

SATURDAY 13

SUNDAY 14

MONDAY 15 ★ ● SUPER NOVA DAYS Relationships turn electric

TUESDAY 16 ★

WEDNESDAY 17 ★

THURSDAY 18 ★

FRIDAY 19

SATURDAY 20 ★ Use self-discipline and patience to overcome restrictions

---

SUNDAY 21 ★

MONDAY 22

TUESDAY 23

WEDNESDAY 24

THURSDAY 25 ★ A loss turns into a transformational opportunity

---

FRIDAY 26

SATURDAY 27

SUNDAY 28

MONDAY 29 ○

TUESDAY 30

WEDNESDAY 31

THURSDAY 1

FRIDAY 2

SATURDAY 3

SUNDAY 4 ★ Talking too much or too fast can incite an argument

MONDAY 5 ★

TUESDAY 6 ★

WEDNESDAY 7

THURSDAY 8

FRIDAY 9

SATURDAY 10 ★ Intuition shows you how to work around the thorniest barriers

SUNDAY 11 ★

MONDAY 12

TUESDAY 13

WEDNESDAY 14 ●

THURSDAY 15

FRIDAY 16

SATURDAY 17 ★ SUPER NOVA DAYS What begins with doubt and isolation
ends with a rush of joy

SUNDAY 18 ★

MONDAY 19

TUESDAY 20

WEDNESDAY 21

THURSDAY 22

FRIDAY 23 ★ It's easy to overreact to criticism now

SATURDAY 24 ★

SUNDAY 25

MONDAY 26

TUESDAY 27

WEDNESDAY 28 ★ ○ You uncover an inconvenient truth about yourself

THURSDAY 29

FRIDAY 30

SATURDAY 1

SUNDAY 2 ★ **SUPER NOVA DAYS** Handle your workload carefully

MONDAY 3 ★

TUESDAY 4 ★

WEDNESDAY 5

THURSDAY 6

FRIDAY 7

SATURDAY 8

SUNDAY 9 ★ Discretion is essential now

MONDAY 10 ★

TUESDAY 11 ★

WEDNESDAY 12

THURSDAY 13 ●

FRIDAY 14

SATURDAY 15

SUNDAY 16

MONDAY 17 ★ High expectations can get cut down to size

TUESDAY 18 ★

WEDNESDAY 19

THURSDAY 20

FRIDAY 21

SATURDAY 22

SUNDAY 23 ★ Getting to the heart of what you hunger for can energize you

MONDAY 24

TUESDAY 25

WEDNESDAY 26

THURSDAY 27 ★ ○ Family secrets may be revealed in an outburst of honesty

FRIDAY 28 ★

SATURDAY 29 ★

SUNDAY 30

MONDAY 31

TUESDAY 1	
WEDNESDAY 2	
THURSDAY 3 ★	Strong opinions don't necessarily lead to effective action

FRIDAY 4 ★	
SATURDAY 5	
SUNDAY 6	
MONDAY 7	
TUESDAY 8	
WEDNESDAY 9 ★	Take some time out to dream

THURSDAY 10 ★	
FRIDAY 11 ★	
SATURDAY 12 ●	
SUNDAY 13	
MONDAY 14	
TUESDAY 15	
WEDNESDAY 16 ★	Unforeseen combinations of facts blast open your awareness

THURSDAY 17 ★	
FRIDAY 18	
SATURDAY 19	
SUNDAY 20	
MONDAY 21	
TUESDAY 22	
WEDNESDAY 23	
THURSDAY 24 ★ SUPER NOVA DAYS	You may sense a profound change coming

FRIDAY 25 ★	
SATURDAY 26 ★ ○	
SUNDAY 27 ★	
MONDAY 28 ★	
TUESDAY 29	
WEDNESDAY 30	

THURSDAY 1 ★ Words may flow like poetry, but details get lost in the mix

FRIDAY 2 ★

SATURDAY 3 ★

SUNDAY 4

MONDAY 5

TUESDAY 6

WEDNESDAY 7

THURSDAY 8

FRIDAY 9

SATURDAY 10 ★ Improve what you can change and accept what you can't

SUNDAY 11 ★ ●

MONDAY 12

TUESDAY 13

WEDNESDAY 14

THURSDAY 15

FRIDAY 16

SATURDAY 17 ★ Slow down and prove yourself

SUNDAY 18 ★

MONDAY 19 ★

TUESDAY 20

WEDNESDAY 21

THURSDAY 22

FRIDAY 23

SATURDAY 24

SUNDAY 25 ★ ○ **SUPER NOVA DAYS** Work, health, and your daily routine are ripe for renovations

MONDAY 26 ★

TUESDAY 27 ★

WEDNESDAY 28

THURSDAY 29

FRIDAY 30 ★ You need to gain control of the situation as fast as possible

SATURDAY 31 ★

SUNDAY 1

MONDAY 2

TUESDAY 3 ★ Keeping your cool is key to avoiding conflict at work

WEDNESDAY 4 ★

THURSDAY 5

FRIDAY 6

SATURDAY 7 ★ **SUPER NOVA DAYS** Manage your expenses carefully

SUNDAY 8 ★

MONDAY 9 ★ ●

TUESDAY 10 ★

WEDNESDAY 11

THURSDAY 12

FRIDAY 13

SATURDAY 14

SUNDAY 15

MONDAY 16 ★ Don't be shy about asking tough questions

TUESDAY 17

WEDNESDAY 18

THURSDAY 19

FRIDAY 20 ★ Overconfidence—your own or someone else's—is a warning sign

SATURDAY 21

SUNDAY 22

MONDAY 23 ★ Apply your increased confidence to personal matters

TUESDAY 24 ○

WEDNESDAY 25

THURSDAY 26

FRIDAY 27

SATURDAY 28

SUNDAY 29

MONDAY 30

TUESDAY 31

WEDNESDAY 1

THURSDAY 2

FRIDAY 3 ★ You're acutely sensitive to language right now

SATURDAY 4 ★

SUNDAY 5 ★

MONDAY 6

TUESDAY 7

WEDNESDAY 8 ★ ● Sow seeds of intention for your year ahead

THURSDAY 9

FRIDAY 10

SATURDAY 11

SUNDAY 12 ★ SUPER NOVA DAYS You are risky and frisky

MONDAY 13 ★

TUESDAY 14

WEDNESDAY 15

THURSDAY 16

FRIDAY 17

SATURDAY 18

SUNDAY 19

MONDAY 20

TUESDAY 21 ★ Overly enthusiastic individuals excite you or drive you crazy

WEDNESDAY 22 ★

THURSDAY 23 ○

FRIDAY 24

SATURDAY 25

SUNDAY 26

MONDAY 27

TUESDAY 28

WEDNESDAY 29

THURSDAY 30 ★ Money matters are on your mind

FRIDAY 1 ★ Your imagination is uncharacteristically vivid

SATURDAY 2 ★

SUNDAY 3

MONDAY 4

TUESDAY 5

WEDNESDAY 6

THURSDAY 7 ●

FRIDAY 8 ★ Confidentiality is crucial

SATURDAY 9

SUNDAY 10

MONDAY 11

TUESDAY 12

WEDNESDAY 13

THURSDAY 14

FRIDAY 15

SATURDAY 16 ★ **SUPER NOVA DAYS** Avoid making serious judgments

SUNDAY 17 ★

MONDAY 18 ★

TUESDAY 19

WEDNESDAY 20 ★ Take your foot off the gas to protect yourself

THURSDAY 21 ★

FRIDAY 22 ★ ○

SATURDAY 23

SUNDAY 24

MONDAY 25 ★ Don't overlook the power of eye contact

TUESDAY 26 ★

WEDNESDAY 27

THURSDAY 28

FRIDAY 29

SATURDAY 30

SUNDAY 31

MONDAY 1	
TUESDAY 2	
WEDNESDAY 3	
THURSDAY 4 ★ **SUPER NOVA DAYS** You easily see how to turn a loss into a gain	
FRIDAY 5 ★	
SATURDAY 6 ★ ●	
SUNDAY 7	
MONDAY 8	
TUESDAY 9	
WEDNESDAY 10	
THURSDAY 11	
FRIDAY 12	
SATURDAY 13	
SUNDAY 14	
MONDAY 15 ★ Hook up with a helpful partner	
TUESDAY 16	
WEDNESDAY 17	
THURSDAY 18	
FRIDAY 19	
SATURDAY 20 ★ Instead of arguing, plan a vacation or a remodeling project	
SUNDAY 21 ○	
MONDAY 22	
TUESDAY 23	
WEDNESDAY 24	
THURSDAY 25 ★ A small task turns into a major project	
FRIDAY 26 ★	
SATURDAY 27 ★	
SUNDAY 28	
MONDAY 29 ★ Your patience for schemers and dreamers is reaching an end	
TUESDAY 30 ★	

WEDNESDAY 1

THURSDAY 2

FRIDAY 3 ★ A simple conversation can turn into an explosive event

SATURDAY 4 ★

SUNDAY 5 ★ ●

MONDAY 6

TUESDAY 7

WEDNESDAY 8

THURSDAY 9

FRIDAY 10 ★ Time stands still to reveal beauty where you don't expect it

SATURDAY 11

SUNDAY 12

MONDAY 13 ★ Words can cut someone to the quick

TUESDAY 14

WEDNESDAY 15

THURSDAY 16

FRIDAY 17

SATURDAY 18

SUNDAY 19 ★ **SUPER NOVA DAYS** You are crossing a life-altering threshold

MONDAY 20 ★

TUESDAY 21 ★ ○

WEDNESDAY 22

THURSDAY 23

FRIDAY 24

SATURDAY 25

SUNDAY 26

MONDAY 27

TUESDAY 28

WEDNESDAY 29 ★ Manage your financial and physical resources wisely

THURSDAY 30 ★

FRIDAY 31

FAMOUS VIRGOS

River Phoenix	★	8/23/1970
Kobe Bryant	★	8/23/1978
Gene Kelly	★	8/23/1912
Dave Chappelle	★	8/24/1973
Regis Philbin	★	8/25/1933
Sean Connery	★	8/25/1930
Elvis Costello	★	8/25/1954
Claudia Schiffer	★	8/25/1970
Gene Simmons	★	8/25/1949
Mother Teresa	★	8/27/1910
Lyndon B. Johnson	★	8/27/1908
LeAnn Rimes	★	8/28/1982
Johann Wolfgang von Goethe	★	8/28/1749
Michael Jackson	★	8/29/1958
Ingrid Bergman	★	8/29/1915
Charlie Parker	★	8/29/1920
Clara Bow	★	8/29/1905
John McCain	★	8/29/1936
Preston Sturges	★	8/29/1898
Mary Wollstonecraft Shelley	★	8/30/1797
Andy Roddick	★	8/30/1982
Ted Williams	★	8/30/1918
Cameron Diaz	★	8/30/1972
Van Morrison	★	8/31/1945
Richard Gere	★	8/31/1949
Lily Tomlin	★	9/1/1939
Dr. Phil McGraw	★	9/1/1950
Rocky Marciano	★	9/1/1923
Keanu Reeves	★	9/2/1964
Lennox Lewis	★	9/2/1965
Salma Hayek	★	9/2/1966
Beyoncé Knowles	★	9/4/1981
Damon Wayans	★	9/4/1960
Mike Piazza	★	9/4/1968
Raquel Welch	★	9/5/1940

FAMOUS VIRGOS

Freddie Mercury	★	9/5/1946
Rosie Perez	★	9/6/1964
Buddy Holly	★	9/7/1936
Patsy Cline	★	9/8/1932
Peter Sellers	★	9/8/1925
Roger Waters	★	9/9/1943
Otis Redding	★	9/9/1941
Hugh Grant	★	9/9/1960
Arnold Palmer	★	9/10/1929
Randy Johnson	★	9/10/1963
D. H. Lawrence	★	9/11/1885
O. Henry	★	9/11/1862
Barry White	★	9/12/1944
Claudette Colbert	★	9/13/1903
Roald Dahl	★	9/13/1916
Agatha Christie	★	9/15/1890
Oliver Stone	★	9/15/1946
Prince Harry	★	9/15/1984
Lauren Bacall	★	9/16/1924
B. B. King	★	9/16/1925
Anne Bancroft	★	9/17/1931
Greta Garbo	★	9/18/1905
Frankie Avalon	★	9/18/1939
Lance Armstrong	★	9/18/1971
Trisha Yearwood	★	9/19/1964
Mama Cass Elliott	★	9/19/1941
Adam West	★	9/19/1928
Dr. Joyce Brothers	★	9/20/1928
Sophia Loren	★	9/20/1934
Upton Sinclair	★	9/20/1878
Bill Murray	★	9/21/1950
Faith Hill	★	9/21/1967
Stephen King	★	9/21/1947
H. G. Wells	★	9/21/1866
Joan Jett	★	9/22/1958
Andrea Bocelli	★	9/22/1958

VIRGO IN LOVE

VIRGO–ARIES (MARCH 21–APRIL 19)

Your personality is detail-oriented and analytical. You're a perfectionist who likes things to be done efficiently. You can be judgmental in ways that become self-defeating if not kept under control. Aries, however, lives a life that's somewhat looser. The Ram is a pioneer who pushes ahead with less organization and minimal emphasis on detail, which can irritate you. You'll find yourself judging irrepressible Aries as juvenile or simplistic, which isn't necessarily accurate. In spite of your great ability to focus on details, you can miss the bigger picture in life's everyday dramas. If the Moon in your chart is in a fire or air sign, you'll appreciate your Aries lover's zest for life. If your Moon is in an earth or water sign, you'll be more cautious to endorse your Ram's sense of immediacy. The bottom line is that Aries are movers and shakers—your life will not be dull if you partner with a Ram. Your sense of stability can help ground Aries, and you can make good business partners. If you can learn to accept your differences, you stand to learn much from happy Aries who can, in turn, light up your life.

VIRGO–TAURUS (APRIL 20–MAY 20)

You and Taurus can make a great pair, for you find a real companion in the Bull, who complements your analytical style with common sense. You are both earth signs and can encourage productivity in each other, especially in the realm of business and practical matters concerning home and family. Your heightened sense of perfectionism blends very well with the artistic and sensual tastes of your Taurus lover. If, however, your Venus is in Leo or Libra, you may have ongoing disagreements about what you each consider tasteful. In Taurus, you find someone who can create an environment that is clean, well-organized, and simplistically beautiful. Your partner will probably pay attention to money—balancing your frugal ways with their abundant desires. Your nature-loving Taurus will most likely also enjoy camping and outdoor hikes, and if they do love the outdoors, they may actually incorporate natural, earthy themes into home décor, including lots of plants and a useful herb or vegetable garden. This is a down-to-earth, no-nonsense match that can survive the toughest of times and thrive for many happy years.

VIRGO-GEMINI (MAY 21–JUNE 20)

Both you and Gemini have the planet Mercury as your ruling planet. Mercury is associated with all forms of communication, so words, ideas, and conversations are lively and emphasized in this relationship. Since you both love a well-crafted sentence, together you can revel in the beauty of speech and music. With all these similarities, you might think this is a match made in heaven, but your styles of communication are quite different. Your refined style is practical and highly critical, making you a talented editor. Meanwhile, your Gemini mate is comfortable when talking without a script, making him or her more social and very charming at parties. If your Mars is in a fire or air sign, you may feel at ease jumping into Gemini's clever conversations. But if your Mars is in a water or earth sign, you may have difficulty keeping up. Wherever your Mars is, you may find it hard to relax around your restless Gemini lover. You can burn off some of this energy by engaging in discussions about books, participating together in literary projects, or exploring new forms of communication. Romantic involvement with you two rationalists is both physical *and* mental. The right words can inspire much passion.

VIRGO-CANCER (JUNE 21–JULY 22)

You are tactful, well-mannered, and have a high-strung nervous system. You find much comfort within the protective sphere of a Cancer mate. You are apt to set the foundation for the home on the material plane by organizing and tidying up the environment. Your Cancer lover will warm and soften your cool aesthetic tastes with photos of friends, cozy blankets on chairs, and emotionally nurturing family memorabilia. The two of you must find a balance, however, because your Crab is sentimental, and in holding onto the past, can create clutter. You prefer neat and clean spaces—except when it's your own clutter, which isn't a mess, just an organized pile. Although you bring a rational point of view to your partner, he or she may not be as impressed with facts and figures as you are. This makes you crazy, for emotionally driven Cancers are more concerned with their gut intuition, and all the logic in the world isn't going to change their minds. If, however, the Moon in your chart is in a water sign, you may acknowledge the supremacy of intuition over logic. Nonetheless, communication flows well between you two; you'll be able to create many fond memories.

VIRGO-LEO (JULY 23–AUGUST 22)

You are very strong within your own self, even if
you present a timid appearance. As such, you are
not apt to need outside encouragement on a daily
basis. And, because you have a sharp mind, you
can be self-critical to a fault. You have, however,
an uncanny endurance that gets you through most
obstacles. Your sharp mind is connected to your
sharp eye, and as such you can be overly critical
of others, too. This doesn't fly with your Leo mate.
The Lion cannot easily take criticism and may be
in need of ongoing praise and attention, displaying
strengths in other areas, such as devotion, love,
and generosity. Your quiet humility may cause you
to bump heads with the prideful Lion, who needs
outward displays of affection to strengthen self-
confidence and courage. If your chart has the
Moon, Mercury, or Venus in Leo, you will be able
to assimilate these leonine traits, using candor
and humor to get around the irritations you may
feel. Your Leo lover can appreciate your razor-
sharp wit, but whatever you do, don't tease him or
her. Handle Lions with respect and honor, even
when they are displaying childlike tendencies, and
you can find yourself in a winner of a relationship.

VIRGO–VIRGO (AUGUST 23–SEPT. 22)

When others are in the company of two Virgos, they may feel as though they are witnessing an elite club meeting in progress. You Virgos can find delight in each another for many reasons. You both see yourselves as slightly superior to the rest of the human race due to your innate organizational skills, acute detail in work, and your ability to execute ideas and put them to productive use. You are amazing, no doubt! No detail is too small to tackle or explain. The target problem areas of the relationship develop when your fastidious minds compete as to which one of the two will rule the roost. You both have set and exacting ideas, but they may differ widely, especially if Mercury is in different signs in your individual charts. If, however, they are in the same sign, your ideas may be more complementary, balanced, and cooperative. This mutual and shared intellectual perspective will allow for peace and happiness. There is good wit and humor shared between you two, but it is usually on the dry side. This relationship may function well and have an efficient practicality, but it's probably not going to be very warm and fuzzy.

VIRGO–LIBRA (SEPT. 23–OCT. 22)

You are as reflective, analytical, and refined as your Libra lover and can get along famously, as long as Libra isn't too wishy-washy when it comes to making decisions. You'll probably get annoyed with the indecision of your partner, who would rather avoid picking one option over another. Libra will feel pressured by you, even if that's not your intention. Libra will feel judged under your critically discerning eye. But it's not just about making decisions. You may also be critical of his or her laziness. And, unless you have Mercury or Venus in Libra in your chart, you'll probably think your Libra mate isn't very practical . . . and you'll be right! Libras are more interested in aesthetics than utility. Your Libra will want the walls painted white because it looks better, but you'll want them a light ivory because dirt won't show up as quickly. Actually, you are both keen on beauty and balance, and can build a lovely environment that others find refreshing, clean, and stimulating. Together, you can be prosperous and indulge in the finer things in life. With some individual adjustments, this can be a compatible relationship with good potential.

VIRGO–SCORPIO (OCT. 23–NOV. 21)

You appreciate tact, as well as a well-groomed environment. You dislike anything crude or unpolished, preferring to relate with people who will not offend or embarrass your sense of decency. Your Scorpio partner, although quiet and deeply honest, may at times step over the line of acceptability for your taste. Overtly blunt, and not afraid to venture deep into the mysterious dark edges of life, your passionate Scorpio mate is driven to plunge into experiences with unedited intensity. Let's face it: you are attracted to Scorpio's frank and honest personality, but you wish your mate could be emotionally more mellow. You will have to get past the manner in which your lover presents his or her views, or your refined nature may feel overwhelmed. Sometimes Scorpio's volcanic power actually scares you, unless you have the Moon in a water sign, like Scorpio. If you do, you will feel more at home with the depths of your partner's emotional realms. The two of you will be honest with each other, and will most likely enjoy diving into the caverns of the psyche as a means of churning up the details of the unconscious.

VIRGO–SAGITTARIUS (NOV. 22–DEC. 21)

Your character tends to be service-oriented with a keen awareness of your duties and responsibilities. You are exacting in the way you deal with the mundane tasks of everyday life and are a great asset at work and at home. The Sagittarius nature is dramatically different than yours, for they tend to be more broad-minded with sweeping goals and ambitions. Your Sagittarius partner is humorous, enthusiastic, and good-natured. He or she tries to make the best out of every situation. Under pressure, you focus on the little things, while the Archer aims the arrow of consciousness into the grand outer world. Your tendency may be to pull in to protect yourself in response to your mate's plans to travel or conquer the world. But if you can get past basic differences, the two of you can work effectively as a team, organizing the details of life with an open-minded awareness. Your chances for long-term compatibility are improved if the Moon in your chart is in a fire or air sign. If you can harmonize your wonderful potentials, the two of you should be able to enjoy the pursuit of shared social and intellectual activities with great interest and success.

VIRGO-CAPRICORN (DEC. 22-JAN. 19)

You're normally hesitant in your actions until you know that everything is proper. Your Capricorn lover is also conservative in action and carefully plans goals and then sets out to achieve them. You are both cautious about matters of the heart. As you tend toward critical thinking, you bring a sharp flavor of communication into relationships. To others, you can appear cool and distant. This works well with your Goat, for Capricorn is also well-guarded at the beginning of a relationship. Capricorns do not wear their heart on their sleeve and can hold back feelings until it appears very safe. Your partner is probably more serious than you are. If Venus in your chart is in Leo, you might find this seriousness too much. If your Venus is in Libra, you may not relate to Capricorn's belief that practicality is more important than beauty. In any event, your organizational abilities should blend nicely with Capricorn's ordered, but sometimes controlling, way of life. For the most part, you'll enjoy sharing the same space and can easily adjust to each other's habits. Romantic fires may take a while to get roaring, yet both of you can be very affectionate and sexy once you've moved past your issues of trust and have learned how to share.

VIRGO–AQUARIUS [JAN. 20–FEB. 18]

You have a very strong work ethics and are a service-oriented type of person. You have a deep desire to help others and are happiest when you're working efficiently at your tasks. Aquarius cares deeply about the greater community and is the humanitarian of the zodiac. Together, you can make waves and have an impact working with organizations, doing most any kind of group activity that involves high standards and shared values. That being said, there are some formidable differences. You are a practical, detail-oriented worker, whereas your Aquarius lover likes abstract intellectual principles. If you can stay open, Virgo, you stand to gain from the "big picture" that your Aquarius offers. If you aren't too critical, you can benefit from the many new friends that your partner brings into your life. If, however, you have Mars in a fire or air sign, then you may actually be as outgoing as your eclectic Aquarius mate. Ultimately, your Aquarius lover needs to relate with intelligent people, and you qualify on this account—you're not only a suitable mate, but your clear thinking can be quite inspiring to your partner. If nothing else, you two make compatible friends—of course, this compatibility can go much further.

VIRGO–PISCES (JAN. 20–FEB. 18)

Sometimes opposites do attract, and there's no doubt about it: Pisces is your opposite. You are exacting and disciplined where Pisces can be scattered and spacey. You are rational and logical while Pisces is imaginative and emotional. You respond to life's circumstances by narrowing your focus, analyzing the details as you figure out your next move. Your Pisces lover discards obvious facts while searching inward, relying on intuition instead of data. If the Moon in your chart is in a water sign, then you'll be more open to the imaginal realms of your Pisces. If the Moon in your chart is in an earth sign, you may think that Pisces is just too flaky for you. You may get annoyed at what you consider escapist tendencies in your lover, although he or she may not see it that way. If, however, you can accept your differences, you can actually be of great help to each other, as you each bring balance into the areas of life that are weak for the other. In fact, you can serve as mirrors to each other's souls. This relationship softens you and teaches you how to become more compassionate. You can teach your Fish how to productively organize his or her life. Together, you can be very sweet and loving.

ABOUT THE AUTHORS

RICK LEVINE When I first encountered astrology as a psychology undergraduate in the late 1960s, I became fascinated with the varieties of human experience. Even now, I love the one-on-one work of seeing clients and looking at their lives through the cosmic lens. But I also love history and utilize astrology to better understand the longer-term cycles of cultural change. My recent DVD, *Quantum Astrology*, explores some of these transpersonal interests. As a scientist, I'm always looking for patterns in order to improve my ability to predict the outcome of any experiment; as an artist, I'm entranced by the mystery of what we do not and cannot know. As an astrologer, I am privileged to live in an enchanted world that links the rational and magical, physical and spiritual—and yes—even science and art.

JEFF JAWER I'm a Taurus with a Scorpio Moon and Aries rising who lives in the Pacific Northwest with Danick, my double-Pisces musician wife, our two Leo daughters, a black Gemini cat, and a white Pisces dog. I have been a professional astrologer since 1973 when I was a student at the University of Massachusetts (Amherst). I encountered astrology as my first marriage was ending and I was searching for answers. Astrology provided them. More than thirty-five years later, it remains the creative passion of my life as I continue to counsel, write, study, and share ideas with clients and colleagues around the world.

ACKNOWLEDGMENTS

Thanks to Paul O'Brien, our agent, our friend, and the creative genius behind Tarot.com; Gail Goldberg, the editor who always makes us sound better; Marcus Leaver and Michael Fragnito at Sterling Publishing, for their tireless support for the project; Barbara Berger, our supervising editor, who has shepherded this book with Taurean persistence and Aquarian invention; Laura Jorstad, for her refinement of the text; and Sterling project editor Mary Hern, editorial assistant Melanie Madden, and designer Gavin Motnyk for their invaluable help. We thank Bob Wietrak and Jules Herbert at Barnes & Noble, and all of the helping hands at Sterling. Thanks for the art and ideas from Jessica Abel and the rest of the Tarot.com team. Thanks as well to 3+Co. for the original design and to Tara Gimmer for the author photo.